A Bornholm Reader

Stories to Accompany Your Adventures on the Island

A unique collection of writing on Bornholm, a Danish island in the Baltic Sea. Whether you're on holiday on Bornholm or an armchair traveller, these articles and stories will give you fascinating insights into this extraordinary island's turbulent history and bright future.

Edited by Tina Hirschbuehl

FLAME POINT PRESS

Published by Flame Point Press.

For permission, requests, or inquiries, please contact tina.hirschbuehl@gmail.com.

Editor Tina Hirschbuehl

Contributions by Jens Svane Boutrup, Niels Geckler, Rakel Haslund-Gjerrild, Ane Ipsen, Henning Ipsen, Bruno Kaufmann, Dennis Gade Kofod, Thomas Kofoed Poulsen, Lars Kofoed Rømer, Henrik Yde

Danish–English translations Tina Hirschbuehl

Editorial and layout Jules Horne, Texthouse, Scotland, texthouse.co.uk

Cover design Tiziana Dall'Antonia-Greger

Funding Jorck's Fond (Konsul George Jorck og Hustru Emma Jorck's Fond)

Citation Hirschbuehl T, editor. 2024. *A Bornholm Reader.* Flame Point Press

ISBN (ebook): 978-1-0687956-0-2. **(print)** 978-1-0687956-1-9

Photos: All photos by Tina Hirschbuehl, unless mentioned otherwise in the caption.

Maps and infographics: As mentioned in each caption.

Captions: All captions by Tina Hirschbuehl.

1 Bornholm lies in the Baltic Sea and is part of Denmark, though geographically closer to Sweden, Germany, and Poland. There are passenger ferries to Bornholm's largest town, Rønne, from Køge (Denmark), Ystad (Sweden), and Sassnitz (Germany). Map: Nations Online Project.

For the Kofod sisters, Susanne and Anette

Contents

Foreword — ix

Preface — xi

Facts, Figures, Timeline — xviii

Part I – HISTORY

1 Who are the Bornholmers? — 1

2 The Strategic Role of Bornholm during WWII, the Cold War, and Today — 19

3 "Russian Days" and their Grip on the Islanders' Psyche — 38

Bornholm in Pictures I — 63

Part II – POLITICS

4 Democracy Celebrated — 79

Part III – CULTURE

5 Of Trolls and the Underground Landscape — 87

6 The Living Landscape — 108

Bornholm in Pictures II — 121

Part IV – LITERATURE

7 How Pelle Continues to Conquer — 131

8 The Stonemason — 152

9 Two Short Stories

When I Started Winter Bathing — 157

The Last Fisherman — 159

Epilogue — 165

Postscript — 166

Acknowledgements — 168

Author biographies — 172

Foreword

By Ane Ipsen

Novelist Henning Ipsen – Calle to friends and family –
once said, *Den bærende kraft i alt det jeg skaber er længslen
efter Bornholm, The driving force in all that I create is
my longing for Bornholm.* Bornholm holds many things
to long for; for me, one of them is the language of the
Bornholm of my childhood. And old Bornholmsk was
not just a dialect of Danish, but a language with its own
vocabulary, grammar, and pronunciation – the word for
boy is *dreng* in Danish and *horra* in Bornholmsk, and
a child's bib is *hagesmæk* in Danish and the far more
evocative *slabbadygg* in Bornholmsk. Like so many other
languages with few speakers, Bornholmsk is disappearing, but echoes of its distinctive melody can still be
heard even in people who have lived *ovre* – or "over" – as
Bornholmers call the rest of Denmark, for many years.

Calle grew up in Hasle. Like anyone who wanted
to go "over" for a higher education, he had to learn to
speak and write in standard Danish, but he never felt he
mastered the Danish glottal stop. Calle was my father,
and I know Bornholm from many stays on Bornholm
with our family. I still quote Grandma Sara, who only
reluctantly left the island, even for family christenings
and weddings. Her sayings in Bornholmsk were vivid
because they were an expression of what it was like to live
one's whole life in a small community on a windblown

island far from the rest of Denmark, isolated out there in the Baltic Sea.

When Calle talked about longing for Bornholm, he was not referring to sandy beaches in July. The charming little towns with colourful houses belie the poverty and hard lives of fishermen, small farmers, and quarry workers in past centuries.

Most tourists visit Bornholm in the summer, and as Grandma Sara used to say in her melodious Bornholmsk, it is Denmark's sunniest island. But if you go there in autumn or winter, you'll meet quite another Bornholm. The barren rocks, the large windswept area around Hammershus, the low huddled fir trees near Hasle, all surrounded by a choppy sea the colour of dark green sea glass. I miss all that, along with the heather, the tall chimneys of the smokehouses, and the snow drifts that, some winters, reached the eaves of the long, low thatch-roofed cow barns, all of which Calle's friend Oluf Høst kept alive for the rest of us in his paintings.

The harsh living conditions in past centuries put their mark on Bornholmers, and on their way of expressing themselves. When the icy east wind from the Russian steppes sent shivers through overcoats and wool sweaters, Grandma Sara would say, *Det e' mæst halkålt, It's almost half-cold.* But for all its starkness, Bornholm will always have a warm place in my heart. There are many reasons for those who love Bornholm to long for it. The selections in this book reflect the soul of the rocky island in the Baltic and its people.

Preface

By Tina Hirschbuehl

Denmark, a Scandinavian country in Northern Europe, is known for its high quality of life, strong social safety net, and minimalist design. The World Happiness Report consistently ranks it as one of the happiest countries in the world. In recent decades, Denmark has become famous for its television, with millions of overseas viewers riveted by Scandi noir crime dramas. And Denmark is inextricably linked to the Nordic concept of *hygge*, a cultural tradition that prizes cosiness and well-being. Hygge is multifaceted and can be many things, from enjoying simple pleasures with family and friends, often by the warm glow of candlelight, to snuggling up with woollen socks, a good book, and a comforting cup of tea.

The Danish capital, Copenhagen, is frequently rated one of the world's "most liveable" cities. According to *Time Out*, it's also home to two of the world's "coolest neighbourhoods" – Nørrebro, and the harbour district of Havnen. But when you've tired of exploring these and other cool neighbourhoods, why not head off the beaten track, to a place that sometimes doesn't even appear on the maps?

The Baltic island of Bornholm.

Yes, you heard right! This rhombus-shaped Danish island is sometimes entirely omitted not just from world maps, but astonishingly, even maps of Denmark itself.

And when it does appear, it's often just a little insert in the corner. But despite Bornholm's geographically marginal position, it's an easy hop not only from Copenhagen, but also from Sweden, Germany, and Poland.

Bornholm has its firm place in the Danish psyche, with many Danes treasuring fond childhood memories of holidays or school trips on the island. A Danish TV travel programme affectionately described it as "our own rocky backyard"; another called it "Iconic Bornholm". Internationally, Bornholm is something of a hidden gem, making occasional appearances in the UK press ("a Danish paradise", swoons *The Telegraph*; "a foodie's delight", enthuses *The Guardian*). As the Mediterranean sweltered during the summer of 2023, *The Sunday Times* even suggested that its readers "swap Corsica for Bornholm", which it described it as a "rustic Baltic getaway". Lonely Planet's authoritative travel tome *Scandinavia* presents compelling reasons to visit this "Baltic beauty" ("the sunniest part of Denmark"), and concludes: "It's no wonder that 600,000 people visit annually – and expect that number to increase, as word continues to spread." After all, who wouldn't want to see with their own eyes a place with sand so fine it's used in hourglasses? Where the rocks soak up the summer sun and retain the heat so well that figs – a fruit quite intolerant to the cold – can thrive.

The island is well known among German holidaymakers, thanks to a direct ferry connection from Sassnitz, on the northern German island of Rügen. On many a Baltic cruise, a stop in Bornholm delights American visitors disembarking on the picturesque island. Hikers take note: Bornholm was once ranked the second-best place in Europe to go hiking, coming after Gran Canaria and before Iceland, according to *Trekking*, a German leisure magazine. *Vogue* admires the "postcard-perfect fishing villages". And trade magazine *Travel + Leisure* describes it as a "new mecca in the culinary community", thanks to unique delicacies created with local ingredients, alongside traditional staples such as *røget sild*, the special Bornholm way with smoked herring. Indeed, the island tourist board, Destination Bornholm, has been showcasing foodie delights in its strategy to market Bornholm as a year-round tourist destination. Fortunately, gone are the days when you had to be actually on Bornholm to enjoy its unique smoked herring: the iconic smokehouses now have web shops, and will post your *røget sild* to various European destinations.

But food isn't the only attraction for visitors outside the peak summer months of June, July, and August. The island's nature, cultural life, arts and crafts, outdoor sports, and entrepreneurial talent also offer travel-worthy experiences during the colder, wetter, darker months. And as the "hidden-gem" travel reviews increase, so could visitor numbers. For several years running, the Danish Travel Awards have voted Bornholm *Best Destination in Denmark*.

The history of the island is as rich and varied as its nature and culture. With little information available to the English-speaking visitor, this anthology aims to fill a gap. This isn't a traditional guidebook, but a guide and companion to what makes Bornholm today, told through its history, its culture, its nature, and its people. It sheds light on topics that mean a lot to Bornholmers, and provides a key to understanding this multifaceted little island described by locals and delighted visitors alike as the "island that has it all". In recent years, English-language books on Denmark have largely focused on the concept of *hygge*. While *hygge* isn't central to this book, it can certainly be seen in the Danishness of the island: each village with the warm earthen tones of its houses, cosily lit behind curtainless windows in the early darkness of winter, is the quintessence of *hygge* – while outside, the waves crash onto the jagged rocks, and ducks and dogwalkers remain undeterred by the icy Baltic wind.

This book is an anthology introducing you to the latest writing on Bornholm by expert local authors, divided into four sections: *History, Politics, Culture,* and *Literature.* Most of the writing in this book has never been published in English before.

To start us off, Jens Svane Boutrup, director of Rønne Theatre – Denmark's oldest theatre still in active use – takes us on an exploration of who the "true" Bornholmers are, in a tongue-in-cheek look at the island's fiercely proud inhabitants, and how they are viewed by visitors from "over", the islanders' word for the rest of Denmark.

We continue with a look at a little-known aspect of Danish history: the fact that the people of this Baltic island only really celebrated the end of World War II nearly a year after the rest of Europe. In 2021, several books were published to mark the 75th anniversary of the departure of Russian troops from Bornholm, but only in Danish. Chapters 2 and 3 of *A Bornholm Reader* provide a glimpse into this time, which is still very present in the minds of the islanders. In Chapter 2, historian Niels Geckler investigates Bornholm's important strategic role during not only World War II, but throughout the Cold War, and right up to the present day. In Chapter 3, through eye-witness reports, journalist Thomas Kofoed Poulsen pieces together a possible scenario to account for why, on 7 and 8 May 1945, the rest of Denmark was celebrating the German surrender, at the same time as Bornholm was being bombed by Russian planes.

For Bornholm, politics is no less important today, notably because every June, it hosts Denmark's biggest political festival, Folkemødet (The People's Meeting). In Chapter 4, we ask a veteran global democracy reporter,

Bruno Kaufmann, for his take on the importance of this type of democracy festival worldwide.

But for all its turbulent past, Bornholm is a walker's paradise, offering scenic natural beauty and picturesque villages in equal measure. And there's more, as we explore in our section on *Culture*. Who is the little red guy on the cover of a children's book on sale throughout the island, and why is he important for Bornholm? Anthropologist Lars Kofoed Rømer sheds light on the island's "*under-jordiske*", whom he calls "*Subterraneans*" – the rock or burial mound-dwelling creatures familiar to every child on Bornholm. For more on this theme, we present some of author Dennis Gade Kofod's retellings of folk tales from Bornholm, although he prefers to call these beings "*underearthlings*".

Culture leads us naturally to *Literature*, where we start by introducing Bornholm's most famous historical literary export, Martin Andersen Nexø. Denmark's foremost Nexø expert, Henrik Yde, gives fascinating insights into the enduring importance of Nexø's works, including his renowned novel, *Pelle the Conqueror*. This provides a natural segue to a piece of descriptive writing from 1967 by Hasle-born writer, Henning Ipsen. Ipsen takes you on a literary journey to a place you might have visited: the hamlet of Vang, with its seaside rock monument marking the hard graft of the village quarry workers.

Our literary journey is crowned with writing by a rising star on the Danish literary scene: Rakel Haslund-Gjerrild, who was raised in Nexø and whose novel, *Adam in Paradise*, narrated from the point of view of the Bornholm-born painter, Kristian Zahrtmann, has been met with great acclaim. In this anthology, we feature two short stories by Rakel – *When I Started Winter Bathing* and *The Last Fisherman*. These powerful, evocative stories weave together a wonderful sense of place and a deep connection between her islander characters and the landscape.

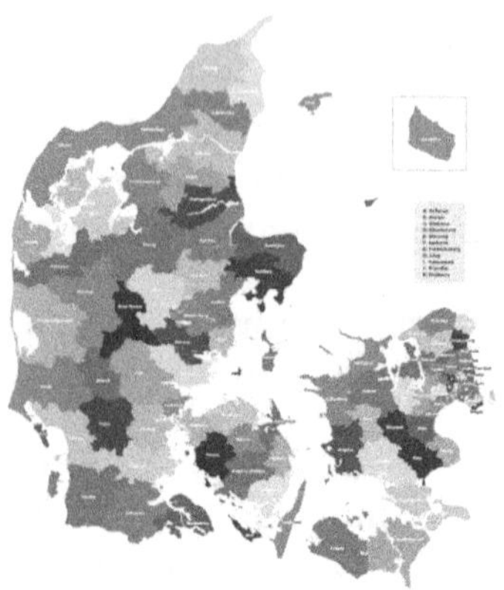

2 Map of Denmark with Bornholm as it's frequently depicted, as an inset. Sometimes, the island is simply omitted. The position of Bornholm on maps is something of a sore point for Bornholmers. Image: Colourbox.

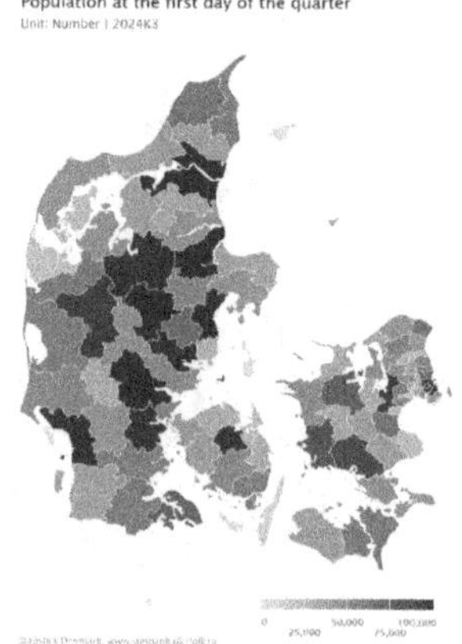

3 Official maps make efforts to put Bornholm in its rightful place. Population by Kommune (municipality), third quarter of 2024. Image: Statistics Denmark.

4 The most recognizable troll on Bornholm, Krølle-Bølle, turns the tables round, putting Bornholm centre-stage and Denmark in the inset. Image: Excerpt from *Med Krølle-Bølle rundt på Bornholm* by Ludvig Mahler, reprinted with permission from Ole Mahler.

5 Illustrated map of Bornholm showing some of the places mentioned in the text. Illustration: Anouk Hufschmid Hirschbuehl.

Facts, Figures, Timeline

Bornholm is an island in the Baltic Sea. It's Danish, although geographically closer to Sweden (37 km), Germany (88 km), and Poland (90 km) than to the rest of Denmark (145 km). Roughly rhombus-shaped, its total area measures 588 km², with a population hovering around the 40,000 mark. Its 158 km coastline – rocky cliffs in the north, sandy dunes in the south – is largely walkable via the *Kyststi* (coastal path), making it a popular destination for hikers. There's also a newer route – the *Højlyngssti* (67 km) – which cuts diagonally across the island, passing through forest, rocky dales, and heathery heights. Bornholm's cultural heritage is just as attractive, with walks leading you through picturesque villages with multicoloured houses and churches in earthy hues of yellow and red, though the island's four iconic round churches are white. And if you'd like to see what the renowned Danish architect Jørn Utzon built before he created Sydney Opera House, look no further than the small eastern town of Svaneke!

Selected dates in Bornholm's history:

1658 Bornholm is ceded to Sweden under the Treaty of Roskilde.

1660 Bornholm is returned to Denmark.

1906–1910 Martin Andersen Nexø writes the four-volume novel, *Pelle the Conqueror.*

1920 Far from Bornholm, the region of Southern Jutland, which had been German since 1864, is reunified with Denmark. Some 600 "reunification stones" are erected throughout Denmark to commemorate this event, two of them on Bornholm.

1940–1945 Along with the rest of Denmark, Bornholm is under German occupation during World War II.

9 May 1945–6 April 1946 After the end of World War II, unlike the rest of Denmark, Bornholm is under a massive Red Army presence for 11 months. "Presence" because it's hard to find a word to describe the Soviet time on the island: were they "occupiers", or were they "liberators"?

1946 Publication of the first book about the mischievous little troll, Krølle-Bølle, by Ludvig Mahler. Krølle-Bølle goes on to become the island's mascot, associated with everything from postcards to ice-cream.

1952 A water tower in the village of Svaneke is built by a young architect, Jørn Utzon, who goes on to build Sydney Opera House about eight years later.

1988 Danish director Bille August makes a film version of *Pelle the Conqueror*, winning Denmark a Palme d'Or at Cannes and its second consecutive Oscar in Hollywood, following on from *Babette's Feast* the previous year.

1992–93 Collapse of Bornholm's fishing industry.

1995–today Bornholm develops a new image as a producer of artisanal regional foods.

2011 First edition of *Folkemødet* (The People's Meeting), the democracy festival that is now held annually in Allinge.

2021 75th anniversary of Russian troops leaving Bornholm; a number of Danish-language books are published on the issue.

2020–2023 The island's tourist board, Destination Bornholm, pursues its strategy to make the island an all-year-round visitor destination.

2030 Target date for Bornholm to become a high-quality, year-round, sustainable destination with strong international appeal, under its 2030 Development Plan (*Udviklingsplan 2030*).

Den lille Klippeø – "Østersøens Perle" – har al Tid ligesom været "noget for sig". Den har til Dels haft sin egen Historie, sine egne Love, sit eget Sprog og sin egen Befolkning, der indtil det sidste halvhundrede Aar kaldte sig "de Fødte" i Modsætning til "de Førte" (de Indvandrede).

The small rocky island – "Pearl of the Baltic Sea" – has always been "something special". It has partly had its own history, its own laws, its own language, and its own population, who until half a century ago called themselves "de Fødte" (those born there) as opposed to "de Førte" (the newcomers, the immigrants).

From an article in *Bien* – "The only Danish-Norwegian Newspaper on the Pacific Coast" – published
in San Francisco and Oakland, California,
Friday 16 September 1910.

Part I – HISTORY

1 Who are the Bornholmers?

Jens Svane Boutrup's comedy lecture, "Bornholmerne" (The Bornholmers), was performed at Rønne Theatre, Denmark's oldest working theatre, in late 2021. A tongue-in-cheek look at the island's inhabitants and how they have been depicted through time, particularly by visitors from outside of Denmark or from "ovre" ("over", the islanders' word for the rest of Denmark). The little island in the Baltic is becoming increasingly popular, not only among tourists, but also among returnees or newcomers from "over" who, during the Covid-19 pandemic, discovered the benefits of the island as an ideal place to work from home. This abridged and translated version of the play gives you a humorous potted history of the island.

By Jens Svane Boutrup

1.

Welcome!

My name is Claus Villumsen, and I'm a Senior Researcher at Aalborg University in Copenhagen. Bornholm's Theatre has asked me to investigate who the Bornholmers really are, and where they come from. What does it mean to be a Bornholmer, and how do you actually become one? These are difficult questions, and there are no easy answers. So, we have to work our way through this methodically, and approach the questions from several different angles.

We can try and establish what makes you a Bornholmer purely biohistorically. We can also look at it from a sociocultural point of view.

Let's start by putting you in the right place. Bornholmers on one side, everyone else on the other. How many Bornholmers do we have here today? Could you stand up, please? Is anyone in doubt as to whether they are a real Bornholmer? Do any of you not understand Bornholmsk? Are there any Bornholmers here who don't understand Danish? Ok, let's continue in Danish, so everyone can understand.

2.

Where do the Bornholmers actually come from? Let's start with a bit of history.

The earliest we know for sure that people lived on Bornholm is around 12,000 years ago. A harpoon made of elk antlers and a flint arrowhead were found at Vallengårds Mosen in the middle of Bornholm, where a group of hunters had lived during the summer. They arrived by hiking out across a long headland connected to Poland, probably to follow a herd of reindeer. Picture it: a group of proud, hardy people, wandering along with bows drawn, and harpoons at the ready. Looking forward to a Bornholm summer – which, in those days, was a balmy 8–10 degrees, but still. Finally, they reach "destination Bornholm",[1] as the very first arrivals. The first people on Bornholm. The dawn of the Bornholmers: a group of Polish summer tourists.

Technically, of course, they aren't Bornholmers. As Bornholm is connected to Poland, they are Poles. And

---

1 Destination Bornholm is the name of the island's tourism board.

the island Bornholm doesn't yet exist, so neither does the name "Bornholm". This period lasts from about 10,000 BCE till 7,000 BCE, and alternates between tepid summers and decidedly miserable summers, also known as the Ice Age. But in around 7,000 BCE, the ice starts to melt, and the headland is flooded. Et voilà: Bornholm is born. Of course, it's not yet called Bornholm, but now we at least recognize its shape. The good old parallelogram. We can hardly yet call the place "the sunshine island".[2] That would be taking it too far. But we can call it "the island". The island that we know and love.

And people start coming to the island again.

Over the next two-to-three thousand years, the island's population hovers somewhere between 150 and 800. The first permanent islanders, basically all of them, at the start, were *førdere* – let's call them newcomers. We don't actually know if these first islanders survived in the long term, or if they simply died out. If the latter, the next lot of islanders are thought to have come from southern Sweden. So, we're very closely related to our Swedish brethren.

In 1896, we find the first islander, the first pre-Bornholmer, preserved for posterity: the skeleton of a girl who lived in around 3600 BCE. We don't know her story, or her name. But she was found in a bog near Klemensker, which is very apt, at least in Danish, as "menneske" means "human". That would make her Kle-mennesket. In English we could call her Klemskate. We don't know much about Klemskate. We can only guess. What kind of life did she have? What was a regular day like for her? What did Klemskate know about the world? Did she ever see the sea? Or did Klemskate live her whole life in Klemensker?

---

2 "Solskinsøen" is a nickname for Bornholm that is frequently used in the rest of Denmark.

Later in the island's history, there are traces of spiritual life. Burial mounds of earth, turf, and stone. People begin to take care of the dead. The landscape is adorned with *bauta* stones (menhirs) and petroglyphs (rock engravings).

The islanders have something to say, and begin to express themselves artistically – an occupation that's still going strong on Bornholm today.

Archaeological excavations around Svaneke reveal Roman denarius coins, bronze jewellery, glass pearls, and other nice things in the black soil. Just as today, the rich prance around with pockets full of little golden amulets, living the life. Unfortunately, some outsiders hear about this, and so castles and fortresses are built, and the residents fight ferociously to defend themselves. The island's strategic location makes it a centre not just for trade, but also for conflict.

It so happens that, one day in 880, Wulfstan, chronicle-writer for the King of England, comes sailing by. He recounts that "On the port side are Langeland, Lolland, Falster, and Skåne, which all belong to Denmark. And then there's Bornholm, which has its own King." And, hey presto, Bornholm finally has a name. Wulfstan probably calls it Burgendaland, and later the island is also known as Holmen, Borringholm, and Borelia… oops, sorry, I mean Boringia. But for the sake of simplicity, let's call it Bornholm.

So, Bornholm is independent, and everything's going well. But shortly thereafter, Bornholm becomes a part of Denmark, or more precisely, East Denmark.

East Denmark comprises Skåne, Halland, Blekinge, and Bornholm – that is, Denmark east of the Øresund Sound. Bornholm is now part of the southern Swedish family. In fact, they've been part of this family for longer than they've been without them. That's food for thought, isn't it?! Bornholm is now subject to Skåne law, while the rest of Denmark is subject to Zealand and Jutland law. Then Scandinavia's largest mediaeval fortification, *Hammershus*, is built, and… no, no, not the Bornholm Medieval Centre. That's built much later.

Converting Bornholmers to Christianity is a bit of a slow process, but, about 100 years after the rest of Denmark, the Bornholmers also become children of God. This doesn't happen peacefully. During this time, while we are Catholics, Bornholm becomes a pawn in a bloody power struggle between the King in Copenhagen, and the Archbishop in Lund.

But on the whole, the ordinary Bornholmer lives in peace for about 500 years. And during this time, when we're closely connected with the province of Skåne, the language develops, too. East Danish is spoken on Bornholm and in Skåne. And we multiply. In the first half of the 1300s, there are 12,000 people on Bornholm. Then comes the Plague, and the population is halved. But later, the population increases again, probably helped by the addition of northern Germans and eastern Danes – or southern Swedes. But outbreaks of plague and other calamities cause the population to dip again sharply over the next few centuries. Despite the cold winters, when people have to huddle up together, the population doesn't increase on its own. Each time, it's the eastern Danes in southern Sweden who come to the rescue, and get the population back on its feet.

In 1525, people start arriving from elsewhere. The Hanseatic city of Lübeck comes to rule the island with a heavy hand. This is an aside in Bornholm's long history, but has a special legacy, as the most quintessential Bornholm surname comes from this time under Lübeck rule. The noble name of Kovot, which becomes the present-day Kofod of Bornholm. We manage to get rid of the Lübeckers in 1575.

But in 1658, there's trouble. Under the Treaty of Roskilde, Denmark loses all of East Denmark – Skåne, Halland, Blekinge, and Bornholm – to Sweden. Now, the Bornholmers are no longer eastern Danes, but southern Swedes! That won't do at all, of course, so there's a revolt on Bornholm, and Bornholm freedom fighters trick (and kill) the evil Swedish commander, liberate Bornholm, travel to Copenhagen, and return Bornholm to the Danish king. Sorted!

Fast forward to the 1800s, where industrialization, and the extraction of Bornholm's raw materials, get underway. The forested commons of *Almindingen* – literally, "all men's"– is created, and the school system established. More herring smokehouses are built, and the landscape is plastered with windmills – not unlike today! In 1900, there are about 40,000 Bornholmers. Just like today. But people are emigrating to America in huge numbers, and so, as usual, new Bornholmers are sought from Sweden. It's during this time that tourism emerges as an important industry. Bornholm becomes the "sunshine island", and starts to tell a romantic tale of a special island, to lure tourists. Starting to recognize yourselves?

When the Second World War takes its distinct course on Bornholm, the island is mainly known for agriculture, fishing, and industry. The post-war population peaks at 48,620 in 1965. But eventually, the raw materials adventure runs out of steam, and in 1990, the fishing industry collapses. The focus on tourism starts in earnest. Once again, it's time to huddle up together. And in 2003, Bornholm shrinks from five municipalities to one.

Not long after, the global financial crisis follows. There isn't much to laugh about during the Christmas of 2010, when Bornholm is snowed in. But in the midst of the hardship, people begin to help each other, and come up with new ideas. Entrepreneurship takes off, and suddenly Bornholm becomes a gourmet island. Now it's no longer *Krølle-Bølle* ice-cream and *fiskefileter med pomfritter* – fish and chips – that sell; now we've moved on to craft beer, gin, whisky, sea buckthorn, hand-churned ice cream, sausages, flour, and much more. The more "Bornholm" the better. And in 2011, *Folkemødet* – The People's Meeting – arrives, putting Bornholm at the centre of democratic conversation between those in power and lobbyists – and occasionally citizens, too. This, together with *Bornholmslinjen*'s low ferry prices, will set new tourism records. With or without a T-foil. Rønne harbour is expanded, so cruise ships can berth, and spout out fumes, while windmill construction helps to salve our conscience. By late 2021, Bornholm has 39,828 inhabitants. And so, here we are now. On the way to new horizons. Europe's second-best holiday island.

Let's recap: We now have a picture of who the Bornholmers are descended from. Who the actual, original Bornholmers were. Their ethnic origins: Poles, Germans, and a lot of Swedes. We also have a picture of how much exchange there's been with other peoples over time. So, although Bornholm is an island, it has never been isolated. And all Bornholmers are descended from, well, *førdere...* newcomers.[3]

3.

But what is it, then, that distinguishes a Bornholmer? Are there special Bornholm features that tell you "this here is a true Bornholmer"? Let's see what the books say. In 1756, the architect and landowner, Laurids De Thurah, describes the Bornholmers thus:

---

3 The original version of the comedy lecture plays on the terms "fødte og førte" – "natives and newcomers".

> *"The natives of the country are courteous, sociable, witty, and mannerly, which is much due to the fact that a great part of the youth, both from the towns and from the country, like to travel to Copenhagen and other foreign places, partly to earn money, partly to practise sailing, since, after a few years, they return and settle in the countryside, bringing back – besides some savings – experience, intellect, and a civilized manner."*

Of course. The islanders' development depends on travel to Copenhagen. Otherwise, they surely wouldn't have become as civilized as described. De Thurah goes on to say that Bornholmers are skilled sailors and farmers, with a great love of their homeland. And they know practically no burglary, theft, murder, or other serious crimes. Their main crime is trouble obeying the sixth Commandment: "Thou shalt not commit adultery"! When you consider how difficult it's been to maintain the population, I suppose it's only natural. The alternative is to import more Swedes...

The problem with Thurah is just that he's not a Bornholmer himself. He gets most of it from secondary sources. But in 1804, Bornholm historian P.N. Skovgaard comes up with an accurate physical portrait.

> *"The northern Bornholmers are large, and strongly built – 67 to 70 inches,[4] with broad shoulders and face. They speak only rarely, and not quickly, and mostly have a deep bass voice. The southern*

---

4 The old unit of measurement used was the Danish word "tommer", which derives from "thumb", and thus most closely corresponds in length to inches.

> *Bornholmers, by contrast, are rarely over 66 inches, quite small and slightly built, healthy and agile, most of them slim, and with small faces, small brown eyes and raven-black hair which does not curl; they are more talkative, and speak quickly. There has been some mixing of late, but nonetheless, the difference is still quite clear for anyone who wants to compare and contrast the Rø-dwellers with the Pedersker-dwellers."*

I don't know if anyone has followed up on this field study. Do we have any Rø or Pedersker dwellers in the audience?

The next characteristic we know about comes from Axel Dam, a member of parliament, in 1928.

> *"On the whole, the Bornholmers seem to be a tall people. I also think they are good-natured and honest, like big dogs – if you don't tease them. There is a saying that you shouldn't have more Bornholmers on a ship than there are masts, so you can tie them to one when they become unruly, as Bornholmers are stubborn, and set in their ways. In general, they are quite conservative. There was much opposition to Almindingen, the telegraph, the telephone, and the railway..."*

Of course, describing Bornholmers isn't an exact science. In 1944, librarian Christian Stub-Jørgensen writes:

> *"Anyone who tries to characterize the "Bornholmer" can scarcely avoid dwelling on his consistently conservative attitude. Of course, that this conservatism has become so rooted in popular description has its reasons. Bornholm's remote location is not sufficient explanation. It is far more likely that new customs and practices are often introduced to Bornholm by strangers, in several cases by force. And at this point, Bornholmers react. There's a deep divide between natives ("fødte") and newcomers ("førte"), and not bridged by the fact that the newcomers often held an uncomfortable authority."*

An important point is being made here. The difference between those born and bred on the island, and those that came later. Several descriptions portray Bornholmers as stubborn and conservative. And this is a significant detail. These descriptions of the Bornholmers are all written by members of the upper class, whether natives or newcomers. And what they have in common is that they are typically the ones who would like to change Bornholm, alter things, instigate progress. Maybe this has influenced the descriptions of the Bornholmers? Is it the case that those who seek change are rarely those most affected by the change? Either way, newcomers are often viewed with a healthy scepticism: what on earth have they come up with now? What do they want us to change now? Of course, you'll also find idealism, tenacity, and perseverance among the Bornholmers. You'd simply have preferred to come up with the ideas yourself. That's perfectly understandable.

For the sake of argument, let's see what it says in the dictionary. According to the *Dictionary of the Danish Language*, the word "Bornholmer" can mean several things: a person from Bornholm, a grandfather clock, smoked herring, a member of the Lutheran Mission, or someone who is cantankerous. If, on the other hand, you look up the word "fører", it's a little more difficult. It doesn't really exist. But "førde/forde" means "to lead, to progress or further"; and "forderlig/førderlig" means "helpful, to help", or "soon, quickly". So somewhat freely translated, a *fører* can be one who is somewhat led, but who also helps or progresses, and chop chop!

In Espersen's Bornholm dictionary of 1908, the word *fører* exists, of course, and here, a *fører* is simply a stranger or foreigner. Someone conveyed across the sea. So maybe we could call them "newcomers". A term for all non-Bornholmers, without exception. Period.

And speaking of the Bornholm dictionary naturally brings us to the language!

4.

The language of Bornholm – or *Bornholmsk*, as it's called in Danish – is probably the most obvious marker of being a true Bornholmer. But where does it actually come from?

Until the end of the Viking Era, people spoke a common Nordic language, but then it split into several languages, including East Danish, which happily evolved locally in eastern Denmark until 1658. But the cession of Skåne, Halland, and Blekinge to Sweden meant that East Danish was gradually ousted by standard Swedish.

Bornholmsk is therefore the only East Danish dialect that is still spoken.

The dialect has more the character of a spoken language than an official written one, and on Bornholm there are several sub-dialects: *Rønne-fint* (townspeak), *Allinge-Svensk* (Allinge Swedish), *sydbornholmsk* (southern Bornholmsk), and a special variant in Gudhjem, for example. Gradual Danification and standardization probably only really started in the 1800s, with the introduction of public schools – typically with imported teachers.

Today, the language of Bornholm is spoken by many Bornholmers, but it's becoming increasingly similar to standard Danish. The Bornholm twang remains mainly in the sounds and pronunciation of the language.

Some children still learn *Bornholmsk* at home, but when they start school, they're taught in official Danish, and the language disappears. However, it stays within you. Like a voice from your childhood. A community between the speakers. A shared sense of humour, and a sense of pride. And a kind of code that can protect you from outside intrusion. From newcomers, for example. But as a dialect, it can also make you feel inferior when you're outnumbered, and today, it's spoken by very few.

5.

And yet the Bornholm community seems to hold a special attraction. For as it turns out, there aren't just many newcomers on Bornholm. There are also many returnees! People who leave Bornholm, only to return later in life. Bornholm actually holds the Danish record in that respect. As many as 55.6% of the 0–6-year-old newcomers have at least one parent who grew up on Bornholm. The national average for this kind of relocation is only around 20%. And as many as 45% of the newcomers who move to Bornholm are in the 20-39 age bracket. So, people of childbearing age. That's promising. The aging population isn't an imported problem. It's the Bornholmers themselves who are getting older and older… and older. They need to get busy, these newcomers and returnees. Otherwise, we'll have to ease up on the sixth Commandment again – or go and get some more Swedes!

But if it should come to that, we'll manage that, too. Because Bornholm is good at integrating immigrants. The main rule is that if you want to come, then you're welcome. Bornholm has several immigrant groups who have settled on the island, and become part of Bornholm society.

Having said that, there aren't in fact many immigrants on Bornholm. In 2017, approximately 3% of the inhabitants are immigrants or descendants of immigrants from Western countries, and about 3% from non-Western countries; so, in total, about 6% of the population. This is low compared to the rest of the country, where the proportion is around 12%.

The low number of immigrants is also directly reflected in membership of the Church of Denmark. In Denmark as a whole, 3 out of 4 people are members of the Church of Denmark; on Bornholm, it's 4 out of 5. That may not seem like a big difference, but it gives an indication of the islander's rich spiritual life.

6.

The spiritual life of Bornholmers is actually divided into above ground and below ground. Above-ground comprises the church and the spirit; below-ground – *de underjordiske* – as we call them here – comprises the myths and the landscape. And neither above-ground nor below-ground belong solely to the past. They have meaning and relevance today.

To start with the above-ground, Bornholm is home to several different expressions of Christianity. The Church of Denmark is of course the biggest group, but there are many others. And then there are all the free churches, and other religious groups. Not to mention a whole understory of healers, yogis, and even the occult.

Jesus has a strong hold on the Bornholmers, too. Just look at all the cars with a fish on the bumper. A former pastor even called Bornholm "God's boxroom".

Let's turn our attention to the *underjordiske* – the Subterraneans. *Nisser*, trolls, and elves can be found all over the country, but on Bornholm, the phenomenon is something special. Here, it's specifically about the Subterraneans, and a close connection with the animist landscape. Here, *Nisser* don't live in the loft but in the landscape, and tales about the *underjordiske* are linked to concrete places; preferably places where there are traces of the past: graves, memorial stones, archaeological finds. For example, you can read or listen to a story about the Subterraneans, and go out and find the place it's set in, and discover ancient monuments.

And it's not all just *Krølle-Bølle* hocus-pocus. The tales of the Subterraneans are about respect for nature and the landscape. Because the landscape isn't just something that exists; it is land that is "created" in harmony between nature and humans.

In a famous tale of the Subterraneans, a lone Bornholmer faces an attack from the sea. A little voice calls to him and says: "Reload and shoot! Reload and shoot!" And after the man fires the first shot, the Subterranean army appears and forces the enemy to flee. Who, of course, are Swedes.

The Subterranean army is the protector of Bornholm, but it requires humans to shoot first. To get help, you must take the first step yourself. There is a striking equality in the relationship between humans and the Subterraneans.

7.

And speaking of relationships, let's look at the one between Bornholm and the rest of Denmark. The place the Bornholmers call *ovre*, or "over".

The Bornholmers fought to become Danish when the rest of East Denmark became Swedish. This deliberate struggle for freedom stands strong in the Bornholmer's consciousness, and the event is brought up when the islanders feel under pressure and let down – for example, during the dramatic days in 1945, when Nexø and Rønne were bombed. The Bornholmers felt very vulnerable and alone.

And when Mols Line took over the ferry route to Bornholm, and the problems that arose in its wake, have led to some people invoking 1658. OK… that might be taking it a bit too far, but it invokes the feeling of being the small one in the relationship. Of constantly having to draw attention to yourself. The feeling of not being loved for who you really are. To start doubting how serious Denmark really is in this relationship. Is Bornholm just a summer fling? Or till death do us part?

8.

But the Bornholmers have chosen to throw in their lot with Denmark – even if it doesn't always feel like their affection is reciprocated. Because if you're serious about it, you embrace the whole package. For better or worse. Bornholm isn't all rocks and sunshine. It's also problems. Even if they're not the things you hear about most. That's a "different" Bornholm that isn't doing as well, that hasn't really prospered in many years. There isn't enough work, enough education, enough money.

Bornholm Regional Municipality has the sixth-oldest population in the country, and the population has been declining over the past 20 years, although it has started to improve slightly of late. In terms of child welfare, Bornholm is at the lower end of the scale for Denmark – typically in category 4 out of 5 as regards the proportion of children in relative poverty; the proportion of children in families with no adult in employment or education; and proportion of children in single-parent families, according to the general vulnerability index.

Denmark has 98 municipalities. In 2016, Bornholm had the 4th lowest income of all the municipalities. It came in 79th in terms of resident prosperity.

Still, we have the largest proportion of returnees, and they choose Bornholm because the island is a good, safe place to grow up in as a child. That's why they move back. How does that add up? One explanation may be that social vulnerability is found in families that have never left Bornholm. In other words, those with the most resources are perhaps those who leave and later return, while the others – the other Bornholm – remain on the island. The same movement as noted by de Thurah in as early as 1756. Maybe those who never leave Bornholm are technically the earliest Bornholmers? Or can't we put it like that?

9.

Now we've discussed Bornholmers at length, and with a certain level of understanding. We have looked at this from a biohistorical and sociocultural point of view. We have come up with some features that we can recognize.

But is it accurate enough? Can we say for certain when someone is a Bornholmer?

10.

Let's pursue the idea of island citizenship. Again, we must look to the west, and see how it is practised there. In Denmark, the citizenship test and rituals are important. In Denmark, as well as passing the test, you have to accept a handshake from the presiding official. Because you might as well learn right away that here in Denmark, we shake hands. Or touch elbows, when times require.

So here on the island, you'd have to come up with your own ritual, to show that this is how we do things here. You could force people to eat salt-fried herring and drink *syp*, our Bornholmer liqueur, but that's almost too easy, isn't it? Now, aren't Bornholmers historically known for being a bit reserved and stubborn? So maybe the applicant, together with an official representative, should sit on a tree stump in *Almindingen*, and be silent for at least ten minutes. That would let you acclimatize to the magic power of Bornholm's nature, and get a feeling for the island. Enjoy the peace. The contemplation.

And then, if you pass the test and the ritual, you become a Bornholm islander. Of course, you're not a native Bornholmer. But you are a Bornholm islander. And wouldn't that be a starting point for feeling like a Bornholmer?

And you could copy the Americans. When you become a citizen, you become Danish-American, for example. So, on Bornholm, you could be a Jutland-Bornholmer or a Zealand-Bornholmer. That's a bit nicer than "newcomer" – isn't it? That way, everyone can be proud of their origins, and at the same time be part of a new community.

11.

But let's try to reach a conclusion. Can we draw a clear picture at all? Well, the Bornholmers' biohistorical origins are Polish, German, and Swedish. And those who are Bornholmers in a political sense are not necessarily the same as those who are Bornholmers in the sociocultural sense. And regardless of whether you use rituals or tests, just because you're a "Bornholmer" doesn't make you a Bornholmer, right? It's not that simple.

We must recognize that it's not only about the label. It's also about the content. The *feeling* of being a Bornholmer. And we have that in common – newcomer or native; whether you live on Bornholm or have lived on Bornholm – the feeling of a special connection and love for the island. To the beauty and nature that benefit us all, and that make us feel so small in this universe – regardless of whether you are a real Bornholmer or not.

By the way, does anyone want to swap seats? Someone who was wrongly allocated at the start of this lecture?

Thank you for the floor.

This is the translation of an abridged version of Jens Svane Boutrup's play *Bornholmerne*. The full version of the comedy lecture was performed at *Bornholms Teater*, Rønne, in late 2021. In 2023, the theatre celebrated the 200th anniversary of its founding. Abridgement/Danish–English translation: Tina Hirschbuehl, 2024.

2 The Strategic Role of Bornholm during WWII, the Cold War, and Today

Bornholm played an important strategic role not only during World War II, but throughout the Cold War, and right up to the present day. This is described in great detail in a meticulously researched publication, "Bornholm i krig og fred" (Bornholm in War and Peace), by historian Niels Geckler and journalist Morten Friis Jørgensen. Some of these points are discussed in this essay.

By Niels Geckler

During most of the apocalyptic slaughter of World War II, Bornholm was a place of relative peace. This changed in the last days of the War, as the island filled with German refugees, and the towns of Rønne and Nexø were bombed to rubble by Soviet planes. For nearly a year after the end of the War, the Red Army remained on the island in large numbers, fortunately leaving before things came to a head between East and West. During the Cold War, Bornholm's geographic location led the island to play a military, diplomatic, and intelligence role far greater than its relative size, population, and economy. It also gave rise to a fairly large Danish military presence, which was a big deal in the small, clearly defined, and somewhat isolated local community.

Bornholm was vulnerable during the Cold War. Evidence suggests that if war had broken out between the Warsaw Pact and NATO, Polish troops would have tried to take the island early on. But this topic didn't dominate the daily thoughts and lives of the islanders, or the Danish armed forces stationed there – although it did become an issue during a number of local incidents or international crises that came and went during the Cold War. After the fall of the Berlin Wall, Bornholm lay for decades in what can be described as a "sea of peace", but units from the barracks in Rønne have been sent on the most difficult of missions – to the Balkans, to Iraq, and to Afghanistan. And in 2022, amid renewed antagonism between Russia and the West, Bornholm finds itself – once again – near a strategic fault line.

Bornholm and the Second World War

After the First World War, the victors restricted Germany's defence, and the upheavals in Russia left a military vacuum in the area around Bornholm. This was about to change. Hitler started rearming Germany, including its navy, which for a short time became a powerful force in the Baltic Sea. For most of the Second World War, however, the Baltic Sea was not a significant place of battle. German troops arrived on Bornholm the day after occupying the rest of Denmark, but for most of the War, there were few actual combat soldiers on the island. Work began at Dueodde on a large artillery emplacement for firing at ships trying to pass Bornholm, but construction was never completed. The concrete structure still remains today.

During the German attack on the Soviet Union, the Soviet Baltic Sea Fleet was sealed off in the port of Leningrad, and the British Royal Navy didn't try to penetrate through the Danish straits. The Royal Air Force limited itself to dropping mines in the Danish waters – including around Bornholm – affecting local fishermen and shipping in the area. The otherwise relatively peaceful sea around the island was used by the German Navy for testing newly built submarines, and training the crews.

The island also played a role as an observation post for test launches of V-1 bombers and V-2 rockets. As the Allied bombing of Germany intensified, German radar installations were established on Bornholm, which was conveniently located on the way to bombing targets in the East. And in the final months of the war, Bornholm played a key role in the evacuation of several million German refugees across the Baltic Sea.

As the Red Army advanced in Eastern Europe, up to 1,000 ships – from cruisers to passenger steamers and fishing boats – were deployed to carry both civilian and military refugees westwards. This would have been next to impossible, if Bornholm had fallen into Soviet hands earlier. It was only at this stage that the Germans attempted to put in place a defence against an invasion, but only of the main towns of Rønne and Nexø. They brought in an additional 1,000 regular troops, but still the forces were severely stretched. The last German commander on Bornholm was the experienced and highly decorated Naval Captain Gerhard von Kamptz. In accordance with his instructions from the German naval command, he refused to surrender to the Red Army until 9 May 1945. This meant that some of the final war action in Europe took place on and around this peaceful little island in the Baltic Sea.

Rønne and Nexø bombed by Soviet planes

On 5 May 1945, most Danes were celebrating the German surrender. The initially festive mood on Bornholm was short-lived. While the rest of Denmark had started celebrating on the evening of 4 May onwards – and British forces, as liberators, began to appear around the country – people on Bornholm were waiting to know what was happening. And when the answer finally came, it was in the form of Russian, not British, soldiers, and only after fierce bombing of the island's two largest towns. On the morning of 7 May 1945, a pair of Soviet planes roared in over Nexø at low altitude, and German ships in the harbour opened fire, though without hitting anything. A few hours later, a large number of Soviet warplanes attacked several targets in Rønne and Nexø with bombs and automatic cannon – a scenario that was repeated in the evening. This time, the planes also dropped flyers calling on Commander von Kamptz to meet at Kolberg (now Kolobrzeg, Poland) the following day at 10 am, in order to surrender. He refused. The Danish authorities and the resistance movement on the island then tried – in vain – to contact the government in Copenhagen, to get it to intervene.

The next day, on 8 May at around 9 am, the Soviet planes were back. This third attack was to be the last, but it was also the most devastating, causing extensive damage to both Rønne and Nexø. Both German and Danish ships in the harbour as well as buildings in the towns were hit. Fortunately, the towns had been largely emptied of people. The evacuation of Nexø had already started after the first bombing, while the evacuation of Rønne started after the second bombing, in the evening. The authorities, the resistance movement, and volunteers helped get people to safety. Suddenly, Bornholm was no longer a part of the "whipped cream front", as German soldiers described their posting in occupied Denmark – and the contrast was stark. A total of ten Bornholmers were killed in the attacks, which destroyed around 500 houses, and damaged a further 2,000 to varying degrees, causing 20 million kroners' worth of damage at the time. Two days later, the first Soviet troops made landfall.

Bornholm 1945–46: pawn in a strategic game?

The dramatic events on Bornholm were part of a larger strategic game. In the latter part of the War, the Western powers and the Soviet Union competed to advance as far as possible on the continent. They may have been allies in the war against Hitler, but trust between East and West had its limits: each side wanted to secure its strategic position for the post-war period. Bornholm was right in the middle: it lay far behind the lines on the mainland where the Red Army had advanced. And the Western Allied commander in Europe, Dwight D Eisenhower, didn't want to risk an unnecessary controversy over a small island in the Baltic Sea.

So, even though Denmark was liberated by British forces on 5 May 1945, and Bornholm is a part of Denmark, not a single British soldier was sent to the island. The awaited reply from Moscow never arrived – but Soviet troops did. Germany had surrendered on the Western Front, but was still at war with the Soviet Union, and so the German Commander on Bornholm did not surrender to them until the final and total surrender on all fronts, on 8 May 1945. Very soon thereafter, the island was emptied of the many thousands of German soldiers and civilian refugees, who were put on boats to Poland, while Soviet soldiers came in large numbers from the other direction. The situation on Bornholm of the Soviet presence, and the Bornholmers' perception of the situation, is a story unto itself. Whether they were liberators or occupiers is debatable. But in the eyes of many Bornholmers, World War II did not really end until the Soviet soldiers left.

The Red Army leaves Bornholm in April 1946

On Bornholm, it was hoped that the Soviet soldiers, who numbered almost 10,000 and were a dominant presence on the small island, wouldn't stay too long. By the end of 1945, the Danish government began to consider whether the Soviet soldiers could be persuaded to go home. The German soldiers were long gone, and there were no tasks for the Soviet military to carry out on Bornholm. On the other hand, there was little desire to upset the new dominant power near Denmark. The British did not want to interfere, and it was not until the start of March 1946 that the Danish side plucked up the courage to ask Moscow – very cautiously indeed – when it might withdraw its forces. And then it happened, quickly and painlessly.

The only condition for Soviet withdrawal was that Denmark had to "occupy the island of Bornholm with its troops, and set up its administration on Bornholm, without the participation of foreign troops and foreign administrators...." The Danish government agreed, rushing to assemble a battalion-sized force to be sent to the island. Doing so was a major strain on resources in the very weak Danish national defence, which was still being rebuilt after its dissolution in 1943, during the Nazi occupation of Denmark.

The Red Army swiftly set about packing up on Bornholm. On 5 April, just three weeks after the withdrawal agreement had been reached, the last Soviet soldier left the island. This occurred a month after Churchill's famous Fulton speech, in which he said an "iron curtain has descended across the Continent", dividing Europe into states that were free, and others that were not. It is not known why the Soviet leadership chose to leave Bornholm without a fuss. Stalin didn't share his innermost thoughts with many. But it was probably because Moscow had hoped to score some goodwill by giving up an island that in itself, didn't play much of a strategic role. The whole of the Baltic coast to the south was under Soviet control, and Bornholm was not easily suited as the site of a major military base. But the interpretation of the agreement between the Danish and Soviet governments on the Soviet withdrawal from Bornholm was later to give rise to much diplomatic wrangling, as well as some mythmaking.

Denmark joins NATO as a founding member

The dream of a new peaceful world, with the United Nations as a body for cooperation between the major powers, and a dialogue-based forum for dispute resolution between states, quickly fell apart. Within a few years, opposing Eastern and Western blocs had emerged. Denmark was keen to avoid having to choose sides, and hoped to officially remain neutral, possibly through a small defence pact with Norway and Sweden.

This turned out to be unrealistic, and in 1949, Denmark instead joined the North Atlantic Treaty (which later became NATO), as one of its 12 founding members. But in practice, signing the Treaty did not result in an immediate increase in the country's security, because in reality, the alliance partners would not be able to prevent a Soviet occupation. Bornholm was particularly vulnerable, as it was far behind the Cold War front, and closer to the new enemy in the East than to the rest of Denmark. And then there was the agreement of 1946, which precluded the question of NATO forces coming to Bornholm. Was it even realistic to expect a NATO response, in the event of a rapid Soviet occupation of the small island? Were London, Paris, and Washington prepared to risk a Third World War because of it? It was impossible for Danish decision-makers to obtain unequivocal assurances on that point, at a time when NATO's main defence line stretched along the Rhine. On Bornholm, there was a sense of being left on its own – just as in May 1945.

The row in 1952 and self-imposed restrictions

Initially, Danish membership of the North Atlantic Treaty didn't trigger Soviet protests over Bornholm, and the only forces stationed on the island were Danish. However, the island's status, and the uncertainty about what exactly was agreed with Moscow in March 1946, caused headaches at the highest levels in Copenhagen, as well as in London and Washington.

In 1952, NATO was planning to carry out Operation Mainbrace, a major naval exercise involving Danish, Norwegian, and British naval units in the sea around Bornholm. The Danish press reported on the plans in the spring of 1952, and soon an article appeared in the Soviet newspaper *Pravda*, strongly criticizing the planned operation around Bornholm. *Pravda* – the Soviet leadership's mouthpiece – claimed that the US was turning Bornholm into a forward operating base, grossly violating the agreement on the Red Army's withdrawal from the island in 1946. The story of American plans for a base wasn't true, and it was doubtful whether Moscow itself even believed it. But it could be used to put diplomatic pressure on Denmark, possibly even on the alliance partners as well. And to some extent, it succeeded. The planned exercises near Bornholm were scaled down, partly at the request of the British government.

The whole affair also prompted the Danish government to introduce a number of "self-imposed restrictions" on future NATO exercises around Bornholm. It meant that Danish units would no longer participate in exercises more than 30 nautical miles east of Bornholm, and that only Danish and Norwegian warships would be allowed to call at the island's ports in future exercises. And so it remained, right up until the 1980s.

Spying from Bornholm

Shortly after the end of World War II, the Danish intelligence services established close cooperation with their British and American counterparts. They built on contacts made during the War, and in those circles, no one was in any doubt about where the new threat was coming from: the Soviet Union, which had already been viewed with alarm before the War. This was the situation, despite the great alliance against Nazi Germany, and the widespread respect for the Communists among the Danish population right after the War, as well as Copenhagen's attempts to maintain a balance between the two superpowers that were beginning to emerge as opposing poles.

In this intelligence cooperation between Denmark, the US, and the UK, Bornholm naturally came to play an important role. During the Soviet military's massive presence on the island from May 1945 to April 1946, it was possible to form a first-hand impression of many aspects of the Soviet military machine, weapons systems, technologies, and so on. The Western powers, in collaboration with local observers, took great advantage of this. Soon, the Danish intelligence services also began to use equipment left behind by the Germans to intercept Soviet signals. They simply tried to listen in on internal Soviet radio communications to glean information on what they were doing, and who was doing it, and to help them be prepared in case they were planning an attack.

For several years around 1950, the British military intelligence service MI6 also used the port of Rønne as a forward operating base in Operation Jungle, which involved smuggling spies ashore in Poland and the Baltics. The spies were taken there in a German wartime torpedo boat with a German crew. However, the KGB knew all about the operation, and were able to dismantle the networks established by the British. On one occasion, the CIA used Rønne airport in an unsuccessful attempt to fly two spies out of the Baltic region. This was in 1955, and it meant that both the British and the American military intelligence services were carrying out operations from Bornholm – partly with Moscow's knowledge – at a time when the presence of US and UK military forces on the island was highly controversial. But the Soviet top leadership probably didn't want to reveal that they knew about the operations, and the matter was not mentioned.

Fleeing from the East in rubber dinghies and fighter planes

Bornholm's location just 90 km from the Polish coast made it an obvious destination for those trying to escape Eastern Bloc dictatorships. Attempts to reach the island were made in rubber dinghies, a hijacked civilian airliner, and even the most modern MiG jet fighters. Some of the escapes were successful; others were not. From a military perspective, the most interesting escape story is that of a young Polish fighter pilot who, in March 1953, landed on Bornholm in a state-of-the-art Soviet MiG-15bis jet fighter. It simultaneously gave the Danish government a diplomatic headache, and the Western powers a unique impression of the enemy's technological capability.

The young pilot, Second Lieutenant Edward Franciszek Jarecki, decided to escape in the jet fighter he had been entrusted with to defend his country against the aggressive fascist Western powers. During a routine patrol flight along Poland's Baltic coast, he suddenly headed north, shaking off his wingmen. Jarecki managed to land at Rønne's small airport. On establishing that he had come to the West, he immediately sought asylum. Meanwhile, the British and American military rubbed their hands at the prospect of examining this high-tech jet fighter that was causing so much anguish as a formidable adversary over Korea at the time. Denmark, however, held back. The Polish government was pressing for the plane's release, and the Danish government was keen to avoid too much antagonism with Moscow. The plane was taken to Zealand by ship, and dismantled at lightning speed – officially, by Danish technicians, while British and American colleagues were allowed to look on.

Only 16 days after the dramatic escape, the plane was returned to Poland by ship, while NATO technicians set about analysing the results of the investigation. This was extremely helpful, as it was the first time an undamaged specimen of the latest Soviet jet plane had fallen into the hands of a NATO country, and the aircraft's high technical and production quality came as a surprise. Later, another two Polish fighter pilots managed to escape to Bornholm in their aircraft.

Constructing a listening post in the 1950s

In the early 1950s, the Americans tried to obtain permission from the Danish authorities to set up a major signals intelligence unit on Bornholm. This didn't materialize, probably because Denmark wanted to avoid provoking the Soviet Union with a permanent – and not inconsiderable – US military force on the island. On the other hand, Denmark significantly expanded its activities in the field of signals interception from the mid-1950s, and over the next few decades – almost right up to the end of the Cold War.

This was done on the basis of technology, equipment, and training being provided by the US, in return for access to all the information obtained through these activities, which were carried out exclusively by Danish personnel. Initially, a small wooden shed at Åkirkeby, which had been taken over from the Germans as a centre for signals interception, was upgraded to a proper brick villa. Various items of equipment were also set up in the area around Dueodde, in the south of the island, and finally, in 1961, all the activities were centralized in and around the old lighthouse and lighthouse keeper's residence at Dueodde.

At this location, capacities were continuously expanded, and new extensions added, as the number of people employed at the site increased. But they were not allowed to tell anyone about their work, and they still keep their secrets today – even though they have long retired, the Cold War is over, and the listening post, as it was called, has long been in disuse.

Building Bornholm's own defence force

Of course, Bornholm's great value for NATO as an early warning and intelligence centre meant that the island would be particularly vulnerable if war should break out between the Eastern and Western blocs. Geographically, the island was isolated from the West, located only a short transport distance from large military bases in Poland. The early annexation of Bornholm was part of military exercises and planning by the Warsaw Pact – the Eastern bloc's joint military organization – in the event of a war. Securing Bornholm would have been the responsibility of the Polish military, and throughout the 1960s and 1970s, they built up a large amphibious capacity focused on the obvious landing areas: the beautiful bathing beaches of southern Bornholm, along with landing sites in other parts of Denmark.

After Denmark joined NATO, the country's defence forces were rebuilt, with US support. For the first few years, the force on Bornholm consisted of units from the Danish island of Zealand (Sjælland), which were stationed on the island on a rotating basis. From 1951, the island was given its own regiment, called Bornholms *Værn* (Bornholm's Defence Force). At the same time, Camp Almegård in Rønne, where the force was quartered, changed its name to Almegårds Kaserne (Almegård Barracks), which is still the army barracks on the island today.

In the following decades, Bornholm's Defence Force was built up into a motorized infantry brigade comprised of all types of weapons, including a squadron of light tanks. As in the rest of Denmark, it consisted mainly of conscripts, many of whom would have to travel over from Zealand in the event of mobilization.

To guard against a surprise lightning attack from enemy forces, there was a small standing force called *kampgruppen* (battle group), which had to be ready for combat at any time. Bornholm's Defence Force would not be sent reinforcements in the event of a war, whether from NATO partners or from the rest of Denmark. In other words, it had to make do with what it had, but it also had the relatively strongest defence force in

Denmark. Fully mobilized, the force would consist of 3,500 men. During high-tension episodes such as the Hungarian crisis of 1956, Bornholm's Defence Force was on extra-high alert.

Although the island's population was not completely unaffected by the anti-nuclear and peace movements that gained momentum in the Western countries from the 1960s, Bornholmers were still generally positive about defence, and more supportive of the home guard (a volunteer force intended to assist the regular forces) than the rest of the country. The proportion of Bornholmers in the home guard was twice the national average. This may be due to awareness of the enemy, a sense of having to fend for oneself, and memories of the Russian presence in 1945–46. Many locals also had jobs at the large barracks, and the military personnel was a constant presence in the small island community. Several of the young men who came over as conscripts found wives and settled on the island, and many officers were active in local politics, and clubs and associations.

Radar on Rytterknægten

While the Bornholm Defence Force was being built up during the 1950s, it was also agreed that the US would support the establishment of a radar station in the middle of the island. The facility became operational in 1955, and in 1962, it was upgraded to become part of the NATO Early Warning System, designed to provide early warning of a Soviet attack. Its location allowed it to see far into the airspace of the Eastern Bloc, making it one of the most important radar systems in the Western warning system. Thus, when Soviet forces, supported by their allies, invaded Czechoslovakia in 1968 to install a government more loyal to Moscow, large parts of the operation could be followed on the radar operators' screens in Rytterknægten, the highest point on Bornholm.

As well as carrying out warning and airspace surveillance, the operators of the Bornholm radar also worked together with Danish Air Force photo reconnaissance aircraft. There was ample opportunity to take photographs of units of Warsaw Pact marines and air forces operating in the area near Bornholm. These useful photos were widely shared within NATO, and to facilitate this work and respond quickly, photo reconnaissance aircraft were at times stationed at Rønne airport.

Bornholm as the naval forward operating base

The Danish Navy, like the Air Force, had a radar on Bornholm. As equipment was expanded and upgraded during the Cold War, this was able to monitor much of the central Baltic Sea. It was an important part of the Danish defence's warning against attacks from the east, some of which were expected to come via the sea. The Navy did not have an actual base on Bornholm, but during the Cold War, there were always naval units on or near the island.

Typically, these were small "Daphné class" patrol boats, which also sailed out on intelligence patrols from Bornholm, and carried out signals interception. Danish submarines also carried out large-scale intelligence missions in the Baltic Sea, and often used Rønne harbour as a forward operating base. The submarines were able to get close to the Warsaw Pact's marines when they were out conducting exercises, and thus monitor their procedures and routines. Or they could lie underwater just off the major naval bases on the Baltic coast, listen in on radio communications and otherwise obtain information on the enemy.

After several weeks at sea in a small submarine, the crews enjoyed being able to come ashore on Bornholm, and sleep in proper beds in one of the island's hotels. In the event of war, however, the Navy did not expect to be able to use the island's harbours. They would simply be too exposed.

A new diplomatic approach in the 1980s

In the first half of the 1980s, there were some changes in Danish diplomatic policy on Bornholm. The end of the 70s had seen some slight easing of the "self-imposed restrictions". But in the early 1980s, there was a major political disagreement over whether an American military band should be allowed to play at the annual Bornholm agricultural and livestock show. In the heat of the battle, the Social Democratic defence minister publicly said that Bornholm was not a "proper part of NATO". This was a problematic statement at all levels, which the foreign minister, also a Social Democrat, immediately had to deny.

The following year, the government changed, and the new foreign minister, Uffe Ellemann-Jensen of the conservative-liberal Venstre party, was determined to scrap the precautionary principle in relation to the Soviet Union. He marked this in 1983 by going to Bornholm with the outgoing US Deputy Secretary of State, who had roots on the island, with uniformed US military personnel in tow – albeit in a civilian aircraft. But now, milder winds were blowing from the east, where Mikhail Gorbachev had become leader of the Soviet Union.

At the same time as the Soviet thaw set in, the Danish government took a stricter stance on the Bornholm issue, expanding the warning systems on the island. In 1986, the large white tower at Dueodde was built, to improve signal reception. The radar installation at Rytterknægten in the centre of the island had been modernized with computer technology in the 1970s. Between 1986 and 1988, the radar itself was replaced with a more modern version. It had scarcely been operational when the Berlin Wall fell, but has since been useful in monitoring the airspace over the Baltic Sea. The listening post at Dueodde was in use until 2012.

Post-Cold War détente

In 1989, after some years of softening in relations between East and West, the fall of the Berlin Wall punctured the Iron Curtain. Shortly afterwards, Soviet leader Mikhail Gorbachev and his US counterpart George Bush proclaimed that they no longer saw each other as enemies – and the Cold War was formally over. Two years later, the Soviet Union was dissolved, and the Warsaw Pact ended. These upheavals meant that Denmark was no longer a frontline state, and Bornholm was no longer located in a strategic hotspot.

Within a few years, military cooperation was established between Denmark, Poland, and Germany, and Denmark provided considerable support for the development of the Baltic countries' defence forces. Several high-level meetings on political and military cooperation in the Baltic Sea were held on Bornholm, and on several occasions, soldiers from the Almegårds barracks have been involved in the training of Baltic soldiers, and the like. But the détente also meant that a large force on the island was no longer considered necessary.

And so, in the year 2000, Bornholm's Defence Force was disbanded as a regiment, despite strong protests by the local Bornholm community, which lost an important workplace and, in many ways, one of the island's focal points. However, the barracks themselves were allowed to remain, as home to a much smaller force, the reconnaissance battalion of the army's oldest regiment, the Gardehusar of Zealand. This force is trained specifically for deployment far from home.

Bornholm's soldiers in global conflict hotspots

The Almegårds barracks in Rønne has clearly felt the impact of the higher international political profile sought by successive Danish governments in the decades since the end of the Cold War, as well as the increasingly militant expression of Denmark's international engagement over the same period.

Denmark has often deployed capacities and forces at very short notice. Often, this has been from Almegårds barracks, where units were ready to deploy, for example, during the early phase of Denmark's peacekeeping efforts during the civil wars in Yugoslavia, at the start of the 1990s. Soldiers based at Almegårds barracks have participated in all the main UN and NATO missions for which the Danish Armed Forces have provided ground troops since 1991, and have received great recognition for this. Since the Bornholm Defence Force was dissolved, the Reconnaissance Squadron has continued in the same vein – and then some.

There have been frequent deployments from Bornholm to the tougher operations in Iraq, not least the long-standing Danish engagement in Helmand Province in Afghanistan, between 2006 and 2014. Some of the soldiers paid a high price for their service. Three soldiers from the Reconnaissance Squadron on Bornholm were killed during their mission in Afghanistan, while others were injured or have struggled with post-traumatic stress.

Renewed tensions in the Baltic

The peaceful atmosphere in the Baltic began to deteriorate as Vladimir Putin increasingly turned his back on Western cooperation forums. Russian military patrols in the airspace around Bornholm were increasing as early as the late 2000s, and in June 2014 – during *Folkemødet* (The People's Meeting), the annual political festival on Bornholm – Russian fighter jets flew over the island in what was regarded as a simulated attack. It was hard not to see this as a provocation, and perhaps a reminder of the island's vulnerable position, amid the heightened global tensions and shock at Putin's annexation of Crimea.

The following year, the Russian military held a major exercise that involved plans for the capture of Bornholm and the Swedish island of Gotland, as well as a nuclear attack on Warsaw – and in 2017, a Chinese warship participated in exercises with Russian counterparts in the Baltic Sea. So, while US attention was turned more towards the Pacific, China marked its presence in the Baltic, and Putin appeared ever more threatening.

The Russian annexation of Crimea in 2014 and support for separatists in Donbas may have strained relations between the US and Europe on the one hand and Russia on the other, but it was not until the Russian attack on Ukraine that the threat scenario really changed, not least in Bornholm's immediate surroundings. The sabotage of the Nord Stream gas pipeline, just 20 km south of Dueodde, really hit close to home for the people of Bornholm. However, with Finland and Sweden joining NATO, the Baltic Sea will be completely under the control of the Western alliance.

Original Danish text by Niels Geckler, 2022.

Danish–English translation: Tina Hirschbuehl, 2024.

3 "Russian Days" and their Grip on the Islanders' Psyche

Every year, on 8 May, Europe celebrates VE Day, to mark the anniversary of the end of World War II in 1945. But few people realize that on that very day, two European towns – Nexø and Rønne, on the Danish island of Bornholm – were being bombed. At the same time, some of the most hardened Soviet soldiers from the Eastern Front were en route to Bornholm for what would turn out to be an 11-month presence on the island. These dramatic events in history still hold a firm grip on the islanders' psyche. In the run-up to the 75th anniversary of the Soviet departure in 2021, Thomas Kofoed Poulsen, a journalist for Danmarks Radio, collected eyewitness reports for his book, "Russertiden. De sidste vidner – Bornholm 1945/46" (Russian Days. The Last Witnesses – Bornholm 1945/46). In this excerpt, he describes that lingering sense of betrayal.

By Thomas Kofoed Poulsen

In May 1945, many Bornholmers were already putting their experiences of the bombings into words: forgotten and failed by the rest of Denmark – a feeling of bitterness that's still felt by some older Bornholmers. And is quickly reignited, if people feel that Bornholm is being overlooked, or that other Danes aren't aware of the island's dramatic history.

Forgotten by the Danes, the government, and the radio

Speak to an elderly Bornholmer about the bombings, and chances are they will raise the subject: Bornholm was forgotten and failed by the rest of Denmark in May 1945. The Danish population, the government, and the nationwide radio news programme, *Pressens Radioavis* all ignored Bornholm. This created a deep-seated feeling of bitterness among the islanders. And it has given rise to a widespread narrative that during the liberation, Bornholm was first left to the defiant Germans, and then to the brutal Russians, while the rest of Denmark celebrated their freedom, and paid scant attention to what was happening on Bornholm. The gloomy lulls between the bombings were met – for people who turned on the radio news – with sounds of jubilation. And Bornholm was unable to get through to the government.

Practically everyone we interviewed spoke about the bitterness fuelled by the lack of help or attention given to Bornholm by the rest of Denmark in those critical days. Even after 75 years, the story remains vivid in many people's minds. The bitterness at feeling forgotten and failed is greater than the trauma over the damage. Some lost everything they owned. But the material damage has long been repaired. Today, no one is mourning a house that was lost. By contrast, some Bornholmers still smart when they talk about the reaction of the rest of Denmark in May 1945. In short, it has taken decidedly longer to repair this trust than to repair the houses. The government's role in particular has been in the firing line, and the bitterness can still simmer just below the surface, 75 years after the events.

Note that although nearly all the interviewees believe the rest of Demark's response sparked bitterness in 1945,

Bornholmers have differing views on whether this has been forgotten today, or not. Some believe that trust has been restored over time. Others still view the Danish state with scepticism.

The youngest of our interviewees were children in May 1945, so they were not fully aware of the issues at the time they happened. But they grew up with the story that Bornholm was forgotten and failed, and can piece this together with their own experiences as children in 1945. Of the around 30 people we interviewed, a small number don't believe that Denmark was indifferent to Bornholm's situation. A few are uncertain. But by far the majority mention some kind of forgetting or betrayal of Bornholm. For many, the issue was that the rest of Denmark celebrated. Others highlight the role of the government. And the way *Pressens Radioavis* handled the news coverage also comes in for criticism.

Finally, in the Bornholmers' experience, many Danes know nothing at all – or at best, very little – of this chapter in Denmark's history. In other words, they see history repeating itself – if, for example, they meet other Danes who don't know the history, or when Bornholm's fate in 1945 isn't mentioned in a history book, or at public commemorations of Denmark's liberation from Nazi occupation.

Jubilation during the bombings

In 1945, radio was the most prevalent nationwide medium, bringing the news quickly to people across Denmark. That's how the Bornholmers and other Danes heard the message of liberation transmitted directly from London. And that's why it was natural to turn to the radio for news in those hectic days. But it was a strange feeling for Bornholmers to switch on the radio after the bombings, and to hear scenes of jubilation unfold on the airwaves, recalls Inger Drewes: "We were standing on the balcony of Tingfogedgård. We couldn't see the city itself, but we saw the smoke rising. We saw the planes that came down and bombed Nexø. My mother and my sister cried and held on to each other, and were so distressed about what they had seen. Every time we went inside and turned on the radio, we only heard 'hurrah, hurrah', at the same time as we were being bombed. That goes deep. We were totally failed by Denmark."

Many of our interviewees emphasized this stark contrast between scenes of celebration, and bombings. The contrast gave the impression that the Bornholmers were on their own with their distress and problems, as nobody seemed to be taking notice of what was happening on the island.

Sometimes, moods and feelings become amplified over time. A sense of betrayal might grow if reinforced by successive betrayals, but that is not the case here. In 1945, these events were already being highlighted in letters, accounts, and diaries. It's notable that several diarists highlight the role of radio in nearly identical ways. According to Else Marie Juul's diary: "On the radio, we hear only jubilation. It's as if Bornholm doesn't count at all. You can't help but ask yourself and each other – have they completely forgotten us?" And Mariella Zeuthen's diary: "The fact that two Danish cities were so pummelled that 16,000 Bornholmers were refugees, and that many of them owned only the clothes on their backs, should go under like it's nothing, in the peace celebrations. We sat and listened, and longed for some understanding and empathetic words, and it's no exaggeration to say that thousands of Bornholmers feel betrayed and abandoned by the rest of the country."

Governor von Stemann made a point of describing the mood on Bornholm when he gave his – often very long – reports to the ministries in Copenhagen. In contrast to many other officials at the time, he didn't just stick to factual and sober official language, but liked to present his arguments in a colourful way. He had himself been evacuated to Hotel Helligdommen in Rø during the bombings. After returning to Rønne a few days later, he described the mood as follows in one of his reports: "It is frankly my duty to draw attention to the issue that, after last week's events, the population's mood here on Bornholm is very bitter towards the rest of Denmark, and the deepest disappointment prevails. At the same time as we heard radio reports about the joy of liberation in the rest of the country, and occupation by the British, Bornholm was being bombed and occupied by the Russians. The population feels that the endless distress and suffering that ensued has hardly been mentioned, or only *en passant*."

The feeling of being forgotten and failed was immediately implanted in the Bornholmers, and this narrative can still be found in largely undiluted form among people who remember the events: "I sent a telegram home to my father in Jutland that we were safe, and that nothing had happened to us. He couldn't understand why they hadn't heard about it. It was awful," recalls Anna Marie Kjøller.

In other words, the jubilation among the Danes may have been happening because they simply had no idea anything had happened on Bornholm. Let's take a closer look at how the news was transmitted in May 1945.

The myth about the radio news

Many of our interviewees point out that the events on Bornholm were not mentioned on the radio news. This is also shown in diaries from 1945. A report from the Air Force includes a similar description of how listeners to the lunchtime radio news on 8 May 1945 heard nothing about Bornholm. The story about the omission of Bornholm in the news programme, *Pressens Radioavis,* has been repeated since the events, in descriptions of the bombings. It has become a widespread narrative on Bornholm that *Pressens Radioavis* didn't broadcast news about Bornholm. This would account for the contrast between the bombings and the scenes of jubilation noted by many Bornholmers. If the Danes weren't told about Bornholm in the news, then no one can blame them.

But in all likelihood, it's a myth that *Pressens Radioavis* didn't broadcast news from Bornholm on 7 and 8 May 1945. *Pressens Radioavis* kept people updated on what had happened on Bornholm. In those days, there were no news broadcasts every hour. There were broadcasts at lunchtime (12:30 pm), in the evening (6:35 pm), and later in the evening (8:45 pm). The transcripts still exist. They show that Bornholm wasn't mentioned in the early evening broadcast on Monday 7 May 1945, following the first bombings of the island at around lunchtime, but that it was mentioned in both the later Monday evening broadcast, and in all three news broadcasts the next day, when the bombings continued, and people in Rønne and Nexø were evacuated. The situation on Bornholm was also mentioned in all news broadcasts on 9 May 1945, when the Russians came ashore.

There has been speculation about whether the news transcripts were not read out, or that they were written by the journalists on duty, but dropped from the actual programme. Only the written transcripts exist; there are no recordings of the broadcasts. But this theory is also suspect: in the segment about Bornholm, the transcript of the evening broadcast of 8 May 1945 refers to what was said earlier that day, in the lunchtime broadcast. It is hardly likely that a journalist would write a script in the evening, referring to news from an earlier broadcast, if it hadn't gone out on air.

In the winter of 2015–2016, the myth about the missing radio reference was rekindled, when first the television station, *TV 2/Bornholm*, and then the local newspaper, *Bornholms Tidende*, broadcast/published interviews with a former stenographer at *Pressens Radioavis*, Rut Andersen-Høyer, who happened to hail from Bornholm. Rut Andersen-Høyer explained that at that time, she worked for *Statsradiofonien*, as Denmark's public service broadcaster was then called. In the course of Monday 7 May 1945, she heard about the first bombing of Rønne, but her editors refused to broadcast the news on the radio.

She recalls that a short telegram arrived announcing that the ferry, then referred to as *Bornholmerbåden* (the Bornholm boat), wasn't sailing in the evening as planned. Rut Andersen-Høyer went to the editors, who told her to report this news, and nothing more. However, she was surprised about the very brief coverage, and phoned the newspaper, *Bornholms Social-Demokrat,* in Rønne. Here, she was told about the bombings earlier in the day. She went back to her editors. They knew why the boat wasn't sailing, but had decided that this shouldn't be broadcast, as it would ruin the celebratory mood in the country. They hadn't told her, because they knew she had family on Bornholm. Rut Andersen-Høyer says that to her great indignation, her editors told her that the news about Bornholm should wait.

It's not clear from these interviews which of the day's broadcasts was being referred to, or how long the editors thought the news should wait. The interviews also don't mention whether the news was not broadcast at all, or whether it only came later. This version of events can therefore easily match the written transcripts, which say that the editors waited a few hours, broadcasting the news about Bornholm in the evening programme, at 8:45 pm.

From a journalistic point of view, it would be very odd for the editors of a large news programme like *Pressens Radioavis* to hold back the broadcast of a major news story. After all, the population had already been celebrating for 70 hours, since the liberation message on the evening of 4 May. On the other hand, those were unusual times in May 1945. *Statsradiofonien* had been censored under the German occupation. It was probably not easy for the journalists to receive accurate and confirmed information about what had happened. The news telegrams about Bornholm from those days were generally imprecise, and contained a number of factual errors. So, it was perhaps deemed better to wait for a few hours until 8:45 pm, as there was a great deal of uncertainty about the facts. For example, *Pressens Radioavis* reported that Rønne had been bombed first, when in fact it was Nexø.

Confirmation that the news about the bombings on Bornholm was broadcast to the rest of the country on 7 May 1945 was provided in 1985 by Tønnes Wichmann, who in May 1945 was deputy commander of the resistance movement on Bornholm. In 1985, he said in a radio report that, after scrutinizing old documents, he had reached the conclusion that Bornholm had been mentioned on the same day. "At 8:45 pm, *Pressens Radioavis* had a short news story about Bornholm's two largest towns being attacked by Russian bombers. Our radio group heard it, and reported it. The reason that people didn't hear it – myself included – must have been the general upheaval of the situation, or power outages or similar," said Tønnes Wichmann. While Tønnes Wichmann and many other Bornholmers were under the impression that Bornholm wasn't mentioned in *Pressens Radioavis*, there may have been other reasons, besides the upheaval, and power outages. For one, the news about Bornholm took up very little space in the broadcast. When the islanders turned on the radio to listen to the news, they justifiably expected the news about Bornholm to come first. It didn't. Some possibly didn't listen to the programme till the end. At the same time, the news about Bornholm wasn't backed by an official government statement. The government could have given the news more weight, but the ministers remained silent.

Also, there were additional broadcasts on the radio on 8 May 1945 about Nazi Germany's total capitulation, but none about Bornholm. Listening to these special reports would have made you wonder. Peace hadn't yet reached Bornholm, so the priorities were undoubtedly hard to understand. In fact, Swedish radio reported the bombs before Danish radio did. It is therefore justifiable to say that Bornholm was given a low priority in the news broadcasts, but it's incorrect to say that Bornholm wasn't mentioned. *Pressens Radioavis* was the nationwide medium, but the large daily newspapers also had a wide reach. The newspapers were already reporting the bombings on 8 May 1945: *Berlingske Tidende* on the front page; *Politiken* inside the paper. The news was not withheld, despite it probably being difficult for the news desks to obtain sufficient information. Telephone communications to Rønne were cut on 8 May. There was no official statement from the government that the journalists could have used.

So, the people of Denmark did get the information. It was probably held back for a few hours by the radio, but not for longer. When the Bornholmers heard other Danes celebrate, this didn't necessarily express a lack of sympathy with the Bornholmers. Even if you heard the news, it would have been difficult to grasp what had actually happened, and to understand the scope of the tragedy, as there were only brief reports, without any official reaction.

In addition, Bornholm was not the only place in the country with fatalities in the aftermath of the liberation. In several places, people lost their lives in various altercations. The news about Bornholm may easily have been lost among other dispiriting news, in the midst of liberation euphoria.

But the Bornholmers were left wondering: "It's really strange that this didn't catch people's attention more," recalls Fritz Olsen. "People couldn't really grasp the combination of celebratory euphoria and then the Bornholm thing. It was a strange situation that was almost overlooked for a few days, but then came the response. There was very good support after that, from both Denmark and Sweden."

Danish and Swedish assistance

Only a few days after the bombings, a large-scale charitable collection for Bornholm was organized. The whole of Denmark was in transition from being an occupied nation, to becoming a normally functioning society. Still, the collection was organized remarkably quickly. As early as 14 May 1945, the Bornholm Committee was set up, and tasked with gathering a collection for the Bornholmers, accepting both money and gifts. The media quickly got the message out to the Danes. Newspapers drummed up support for the collection. Local committees were created, helping the initiative to reach the population up and down the country. People put up posters in Copenhagen. Cinema screenings, football matches, and lotteries were held to benefit the Bornholmers. Children sold their toys to raise money.

Through the Bornholm Committee, helping the Bornholmers became a national cause. By late May 1945, this was the main topic of conversation in workplaces and shops. The volunteers were rushed off their feet. The telephone lines ran hot with people wanting to help the Bornholmers. During course of May, over 2 million kroner was already collected, rising later to 7.6 million kroner. And then there were gifts of clothing, household items, and furniture. Eleven shiploads were sent from Copenhagen to Bornholm.

Inger Drewes watched from the sidelines, as the numerous items arrived in Nexø: "We got a lot of help from the Swedes, and when the Danes realized what had happened, they sent over clothing and furniture. Considering that there had been war for five years, they really sent us a lot. It was stored in Nexø. My mother was up there to help them distribute it," Inger Drewes remembers.

It's worth noting that she mentions the Swedish support in the same breath as Danish support. In Sweden, there was also a collection of money for Bornholm, but even more importantly: as early as May 1945, the Swedish state offered to provide wooden houses for Rønne and Nexø, to solve the housing shortage. A total of 225 wooden houses were built in Rønne, and 75 in Nexø. When talking about the reconstruction, other older Bornholmers highlight the support from Sweden and not Denmark, despite the Danish assistance being greater.

These "Swedish Houses" still stand as charismatic and eye-catching houses in both Rønne and Nexø. Entire streets were built, with rows of identical houses in many different colours. They are still attractive and generally well-kept houses. So, it's perhaps not surprising that some Bornholmers are inclined to recall only the reconstruction support granted by Sweden. Their visibility in the townscape reminds people about the Swedes' gift even 75 years later, whereas Denmark's assistance is less visible today, even though it was both quick and effective. The Danish state provided economic assistance in various different ways. For example, it helped pay for the construction of the Swedish houses. In addition, the state supported other initiatives, such as architectural support to ensure the reconstruction fitted harmoniously into the townscape in Rønne and Nexø.

The Foreign Ministry didn't want to be disturbed

The enthusiastic and rapid efforts to support the reconstruction didn't erase the feelings of bitterness felt by many Bornholmers. While some attribute this to the radio news and the population's celebrations, others single out the role of the government. This story centres on Foreign Minister Christmas Møller's failure to answer the phone on the evening of Monday 7 May 1945 – a time of real crisis, as the Russians had dropped flyers warning of new attacks the following day. Both the resistance movement and Governor von Stemann called the Foreign Ministry several times, to ask Christmas Møller to pull some strings and stop the Russians. The deputy commander in the resistance movement, Tønnes Wichmann, described the experience as follows: "We got through to a secretary in the Foreign Ministry, but were told that Foreign Minister Christmas Møller was in a meeting, and was not to be disturbed. We kept trying. I think we rang every half hour. Finally, at around 10 pm, we were told that the Foreign Minister had gone home. We got his private number. We called his private number, and were told that he had gone to bed, and was not to be disturbed," said Tønnes Wichmann, in a radio report in 1985.

This lack of response has not been forgotten on Bornholm. Lars Peter Dahl still remembers it clearly: "We were bitter about the government for that. People think back to the poor leadership of the country – Christmas Møller in particular. People of my age will never forget that," he says. Bjarne Ilsted Bech believes that this still influences the island's older generation: "When the government learnt that there were problems over here, nobody wanted to touch the issue. It was a hot potato that was passed from one person to the next. I'm sure this caused a lot of anger and dissatisfaction among many people. I think it's still deep-seated among some."

By being out of reach that Monday evening, Christmas Møller came to symbolize the government's unwillingness to solve the problem, and its disinterest in Bornholm. The anger on Bornholm was aimed at the Foreign Minister personally. It was interpreted as arrogance, passivity, and indifference over the island's fate. Christmas Møller later expressed regret at the situation. He explained that he hadn't been called to the telephone by the secretary at the Foreign Ministry. Before the bombings, people on Bornholm had wondered why the British allies had not yet come to the island to accept the German capitulation. As late as 7 May 1945, and after the first bombs had fallen, the German Commander, von Kamptz, had restated to the resistance movement that he wanted to surrender to the British allies. That same evening, Governor von Stemann again asked Copenhagen to send a British representative to the island. Many asked themselves why the government hadn't arranged this.

For many years after 1945, why the British allies didn't come was a bit of a mystery, giving rise to myths and speculation about the issue. Maybe the British didn't know that Bornholm belonged to Denmark? Others believed that Bornholm was located too far east, behind some secret lines on the map, and lay within Russian territory. The highest commander of the British forces in Denmark in 1945, General Dewing, didn't do anything to clear up the mystery. On the contrary – many years after the war, Dewing claimed in an interview that there hadn't been the military capacity to liberate Bornholm. That wasn't true, either, but it contributed to the perception that Bornholm had been overlooked.

In long articles marking the 25th anniversary of the liberation in 1970, the island's newspaper, *Bornholms Tidende*, wrote that the mystery would only be solved in the next century. But it wasn't to take that long. After the end of the Cold War in the 1990s, access was granted to more documents, but it took several decades to get a satisfactory explanation for Bornholm's fate. That's why many explanations given for the situation in 1945 were not necessarily correct or comprehensive, and the image of a weak Danish government was not given enough nuance. On many key points, both the Foreign Minister and the Prime Minister were blameless, and couldn't have acted much more effectively than they did.

In 1996, historian Bent Jensen published a book called *Den lange befrielse* (*The Long Liberation*), in which he describes what happened in detail: the British had been asked to stay away from Bornholm by US General Eisenhower, who was Supreme Commander of the Allied Expeditionary Force in Europe. Bornholm had been marked in red on the military's strategic road map, which was followed by the British on their way into Denmark. In short, Bornholm was off limits. And a rumour circulated among the Americans that the Russians had set their sights on the island. That's why Eisenhower didn't want to risk provoking the Russians. Bornholm was not at all forgotten during the liberation. On the contrary, military headquarters had full attention on the island. However, it could be said that the Allies had omitted to clarify among themselves who was to travel to Bornholm. That's according to the rumours. There was no agreement between them about the liberation of Bornholm in advance.

At the same time, it is documented that the Danish government did act to prevent further attacks on Rønne and Nexø, despite the government being entirely new, and still without established diplomatic relations with the Soviet Union. The Foreign Minister, Christmas Møller, only arrived in Denmark from exile in London on Monday 7 May 1945, just before noon – at around the same time as the first bombs hit Nexø. That Monday lunchtime, Prime Minister Vilhelm Buhl approached General Dewing for help. The British General took the issue to Eisenhower, who turned to the Russians, to ask if sending a British representative to Bornholm would conflict with the Russians' plans. The Russians didn't reply straight away, but chose to enter Bornholm themselves.

Contrary to what the resistance movement had been told, Christmas Møller didn't go to bed early. Late on 7 May 1945, at 11:30 pm, he discussed Bornholm with envoy Kruse in Stockholm, asking the envoy to help solve the problem of the Russian ultimatum. This was because the government didn't have direct relations with the Soviet Union, and therefore had to try via other channels. Something was being done, but the Danish government had no other scope for action. The question of Bornholm's fate lay on the Great Powers' chessboard. And the Danish government couldn't so much as whisper into the players' ears, even though it would have liked to.

In terms of how he was perceived by Bornholmers, Christmas Møller didn't make it easier for himself by, for example, giving a radio speech on 9 May 1945 in which he praised the Soviet Union and Stalin, and sent warm thanks to the eastern neighbour for participating in Denmark's liberation – notably, without a single mention of Bornholm. Neither was Bornholm mentioned when Parliament reopened on 9 May 1945. Apparently, the government was very nervous about saying anything that could provoke the Russians. They therefore chose to stay silent on Bornholm's unresolved and critical situation. The strategy was to thank the Russians in the short term, in order to be able to negotiate with them to secure Danish sovereignty over Bornholm in the long term. At the same time, it is worth noting that the government didn't approach Bornholm at any time during this critical period between the first and last bombings – a failure in communication. On Bornholm, this naturally contributed to the perception of Bornholm having been forgotten.

The combination of the government's silence on the issue, the very brief news telegrams, and a jubilant population in the rest of Denmark, resulted in the Bornholmers beginning to doubt their sense of national belonging. In May 1945, the Freedom Council's local committee on Bornholm wrote letters to Copenhagen and to King Christian X, pleading for help to ensure that Bornholm would remain a part of the Kingdom of Denmark. Bornholmers today still remember this: "If you belong to Denmark, then you belong to Denmark. In that case, it's no good that they were celebrating wildly in Copenhagen, while we were being showered with bombs. After that, we were mistrustful of people from Copenhagen," says Erling Pedersen.

Lis Ellegaard remembers how, in her home, a question mark arose around Bornholm's sense of national belonging: "The Danes should have been more interested in what was happening, instead of celebrating. We felt completely forgotten. I remember that my father said he'd rather belong to Sweden. That's how deep the disappointment was."

In the streets of Rønne, Governor von Stemann picked up on doubt about the sense of national belonging. In one of his briefings to Copenhagen in May 1945, he reported hearing people say they wished the Bornholmers had never shot the Swedish Commander Printzenskjöld in 1658 and returned the island to Denmark.

At the Treaty of Roskilde in 1658 between Denmark and Sweden, Bornholm was ceded to the Swedes, but the Bornholmers liberated the island later in the year, by shooting the Swedish commander in cold blood, in Storegade in Rønne. A Bornholm delegation later agreed with the King that the island should become Danish again, in return for certain privileges, such as in relation to taxation. In 1658, Bornholm had been transferred to a foreign power, but it was the Bornholmers themselves who chose to belong to Denmark, and they got something in return.

The feeling persists

Traces of mistrust towards Copenhagen can still be found among Bornholmers today. Some believe that trust has been rebuilt over time. Others draw the same historical parallels to 1658 as the governor noted in 1945. Some Bornholmers today see the reaction from Copenhagen in May 1945 as part of a recurring pattern. The experience of 1945 recalls the events around the Treaty of Roskilde in 1658 – and still reverberates in current political events.

In other words, we can draw on the events of 1658 and 1945 in current political debates, by pointing out that Bornholm is again being overlooked. More recent examples of the perception of Bornholm having been forgotten or treated unfairly can be seen in issues such as the ferry connection to and from Bornholm, or the indifference to placing Bornholm correctly onto the map: "The Bornholmers took action to ensure their return to Denmark, and then you see, time and again, that Bornholm just doesn't count, in the rest of the country," says Preben Miland Grönvald.

The rationale seems to be that both sides have a responsibility, when it comes to the national sense of belonging. Just as the Bornholmers committed to being a part of Denmark back in 1658, so must the Danish state also be committed to Bornholm. And when people perceive this not to be the case, they bring up history. Today, very few Bornholmers would probably prefer to be Swedish citizens, but the debate on the sense of national belonging is ongoing. For some Bornholmers, the experience of 1945 has strengthened their wish for more regional autonomy or self-governance – a wish that originates from mistrust of the state: "I would rather be governed by Brussels than by Copenhagen. Because in Brussels, it's so big that they have to put many decisions out to the regions, but in Copenhagen, they want to micro-manage us," says Carl Aage Reuss.

On the other hand, there are also Bornholmers who believe that the bitterness no longer has any meaning. Fritz Olsen thinks the conflict has been settled over time: "People celebrated in Denmark without Bornholm. Some things were a bit contradictory, but I don't think there's all that much left of that." Erna Kofoed feels she's heard enough about the bitterness over the last 75 years: "The Bornholmers talk a lot about being failed. Now stop talking about it. They should be allowed to be happy in Copenhagen. What good does our bitterness do? Of course it was too bad, but surely they should be allowed to be happy."

Some Bornholmers also believe that the feeling of bitterness will die out with their generation. The younger generations aren't caught between the same feelings, because they didn't experience the bombings themselves. Some participants mentioned that older members of their family were very upset about the issue in 1945, but they themselves weren't as bitter. It's a generational issue, says Aly Svendsen: "The feeling is still there. It's only the younger people that don't think about it, but with the older ones, the idea that the Danes completely forgot us is still in there somewhere."

Nobody knows anything today

Practically everyone we interviewed agreed that most Danes know nothing – or at best, very little – about the distinct Bornholm version of the end of the Second World War. Nearly everyone has personal experiences of meeting Danes who knew nothing about the bombings: "Usually people don't know a thing about it. When I have guests here, I always ask if they've been over at the Russian cemetery. Then I can see from their expression what they know," says Anders Koefoed Larsen from Allinge, who lives near the graveyard for Russian soldiers.

Most of the participants find it lamentable that knowledge of the history is, in their view, generally low. A few of them say it's understandable, with so many other events since 1945, both in Denmark and abroad, competing for attention. Some people compare this to their parents being able to remember the First World War – a part of history they themselves have never related to in the same way.

But most are unhappy about many Danes not knowing this part of Bornholm's history. For Per Samuelsen, this lack of knowledge is hurtful: "This is still a sore point for my generation. It's connected to the fact that so many people in the rest of the country don't know anything about it," he explained. Niels Clausen sees this lack of knowledge as an expression of official Denmark not being proud of what happened back then. They are like two sides of the same coin: today's lack of knowledge, and, back then, the sense of being failed and forgotten: "Many don't know much about the fact that we had Russians on Bornholm. Many don't have even an inkling, and don't know that we were bombed. They know very little, but the government also hasn't been good at telling people about it. It's as if it was also a dark chapter for them."

Many Bornholmers point to the public school system for not prioritizing the subject and the events in history lessons, lamenting that teachers are also uninformed about it: "It's become worrying now. Not long ago I was chatting with a school teacher who was around 40. We were at the public swimming pool. He didn't know a thing about the War. That's too bad for Denmark," says Erling Pedersen.

In the 1980s, the former Bornholm Member of Parliament Niels Anker Kofoed said he had complained to the Education Minister about the subject not being taught in schools. The matter is not that simple, and is slightly reminiscent of the situation with *Pressens Radioavis*. In the 1998 book *Historien fortalt* (History Told), author Torben Weinreich analyses eight public school history books from the 1980s and 1990s. All books mention the bombings and the occupation of Bornholm, albeit quite briefly. Still, it's not certain that history teachers have used the pages about Bornholm in their lessons. And if they did, it's not certain that they made a lasting impression upon the students.

This chapter has shown that the Bornholmers still remember the sense of betrayal they felt in May 1945. The nuances of the events at the time, especially around the radio news and the role of the government which emerged after the events, hasn't erased all bitterness. This might be partly due to some Bornholmers today feeling that the island is also overlooked in other matters, and many having met Danes who are unaware of the history. Thus the experience of being forgotten and failed in May 1945 is repeated.

The question is whether time will heal the last remaining rifts from the wounds of bitterness of 1945, or whether the story of Denmark's betrayal will be passed on to the next generations of Bornholmers, and live on as a strong regional narrative, in the same way as the story of the 1658 uprising against the Swedes. This will become clear in the coming decades. However, there are indications that this may indeed be the case: Bornholmers have an increasing tendency to emphasize special characteristics of the island's history. And since 1945, they have gradually distanced themselves from the Danish traditions surrounding the celebration of Denmark's liberation on 4 May 1945, because of the particular course taken by the end of World War II on Bornholm.

Chapter References

Jubilation during the bombings

- Else Marie Juul and Mariella Zeuthen's diaries (www. bornholmskebilleder.dk)

- The Governor's report is from *En dansk embedsmands odysée II* (p. 140).

The myth about the radio news

- There are many reports of Pressens Radioavis not mentioning the bombings. E.g. Børge Kure's collection of articles, *En ø i krig* (p. 15), the TV documentary Bornholm, befriet og bombet (8 May 1985, DR's archive), and Bornholms Tidende, 4 May 1965.

- *Pressens Radioavis* scripts are from the archive of Det Kongelige Bibliotek (Royal Danish Library).

- Speculations that the manuscripts were not read on air are from Jesper Gaarskjær's book *Bornholm besat* (p. 66).

- Rut Andersen-Høyer appeared on TV 2/Bornholm on 26 October 2015, and in *Bornholms Tidende* on 9 January 2016.

- Comments about the prioritization of news in *Pressens Radioavis* and censoring is from an interview with editor Thomas Jensen in *Bornholms Tidende*, on 27 January 2016.

- Tønnes Wichmann appeared in the radio programme *Bornholm befriet og bombet* (8 May 1985, DR's archive).

- Jacob Hornemann writes in *Bornholm mellem Øst og Vest* that Swedish radio broadcast the news about Bornholm on 7 May 1945, at 8 pm, i.e. around 45 minutes before Danish radio.

- The prioritization of news in *Pressens Radioavis* is described by Jesper Gaarskjær in his book *Bornholm besat* (p. 66).

- The fact that the telephone connection was interrupted comes from Governor von Stemann's memoirs (pp. 122 and 126) and Børge Kure's *En ø i Krig* (p. 14).

- The news reported by the nationwide newspapers can be read in *Politiken* and *Berlingske Tidende* of 8 May 1945.

Danish and Swedish assistance

- The paragraph about the charitable collection is from Bornholmskomiteen 1952: *Hjælp til Rønne og Nexø* (pp. 24–28). The information about the Swedish Houses comes from the same book (pp. 32, 40–44).

- Thomas Jensen's *Bornholm 1945* (*Bornholms Tidendes Forlag* 1995) also describes the assistance to Bornholm, including architectural assistance.

The Foreign Ministry didn't want to be disturbed

- The attempts to contact the Foreign Ministry are described in Jacob Hornemann's *Bornholm mellem Øst og Vest*.

- The quotes by Tønnes Wichmann are from the TV documentary *Bornholm, befriet og bombet* (8 May 1985, DR's archive). The explanations about the reasons for trying to contact the Foreign Ministry are from the radio programme, *Bornholm befriet og bombet* (8 May 1985, DR's archive).

- Christmas Møller's role is described by Bent Jensen in *Den lange befrielse* (pp. 99 and 110).

- The mystery and myths surrounding the actions by the British is described by Bent Jensen in *Den lange befrielse* (p. 15) and in *Bornholms Tidende* (2 May 1970). The explanation about General Dewing is from p. 79 in Bent Jensen's book.

- The instruction that a British representative would not be sent to Bornholm is described by Bent Jensen in *Den lange befrielse* (pp. 68–73). Other explanations for the Danish government's decisions are found on pp.104–106. The government not approaching Bornholm is mentioned on p. 112.

- The government being nervous about provoking the Russians is mentioned in the radio programme, *Bornholm befriet og bombet* (8 Mai 1945, DR's archive).

- The Governor's report of 14 May 1945 is mentioned in Jacob Hornemann, *Bornholm mellem Øst og Vest.*

Nobody knows anything today

- Torben Weinreich's book, *Historien fortalt* (Samfundsliteratur 1998) contains an analysis of history books in state schools.

- Niels Anker Kofod's complaint to the education ministry is described in Øyvind Kyrø's book, *Det hemmelige Bornholm* (People's Press 2017).

Original Danish text: Poulsen, Thomas Kofoed. 2021. "Bornholm blev glemt og bliver det stadig" (Kapitel 4) *In*: Poulsen, TK. 2021. *Russertiden. De sidste vidner – Bornholm 1945/46*. Rønne: Hakon Holm Publishing, pp. 55–72.
Danish–English translation: Tina Hirschbuehl, 2024.

Bornholm in Pictures I

6 The enigmatic little golden amulets, or gold foil figures, called *guldgubber* in Danish, are actually something of an archaeological sensation. They were found in 25 different Nordic locations, with by far the greatest find on Bornholm. A whopping 2,300 were found in the Sorte Muld (Black Soil) area. These days, you can buy a replica as a pendant (pictured) at Bornholm's Museum. Photo: Manon Hufschmid Hirschbuehl.

7 Hasle Smokehouse, open for lunch and dinner all year round. Nearly every coastal town on Bornholm has a smokehouse, although many are no longer open during the winter.

8 The popular story of *Krølle-Bølle* was first published in 1946 by Ludvig Mahler. In 2020, a special edition was issued in Bornholmsk by Ludvig's son, Ole Mahler.

9 There are 22 churches on Bornholm, four of which are round.
Top left: Østerlars Rundkirke.
Right: Svaneke Kirke.
Bottom: Povls Kirke (Poulsker).
The ending "-ker" is short for "kirke" (church).

10 Nothing says "Bornholm" more than stones and trolls. You might find an unmanned roadside stall where you can pick one up, if you have Mobilepay.

11 This photo of gas leaking from the Nord Stream 2 pipeline in the Baltic Sea – off the coast of Bornholm – was used by most of the world's media in October 2022. And suddenly, Bornholm was not just on the Danish, but also on the world map. Photo: Danish Defence.

12 Still there: a large artillery emplacement in the woods near Dueodde, built by German troops on Bornholm during WWII. Construction was never completed, but the structure remains.

13 The new lighthouse at Dueodde. Operational since 1962, it replaced the old lighthouse mentioned in Chapter 2.

14 Left: The large white tower at Dueodde was built in 1986 to improve signal reception; the Berlin Wall was to fall three years later. Below: The small round stone tower is the old lighthouse, which became the hub of Cold War monitoring activities in 1961. The site is now a privately owned museum.

15 Oh, so that's where Bornholm is! This infographic was one of many published by media outlets across the globe in October 2022. Infographic: Anadolu Images.

16 Despite Danish assistance to Bornholm after the bombings of Rønne and Nexø being quick and effective, it's the "Swedish Houses", still so visible in the townscape, that people remember.

17 The graveyard for Russian soldiers in Allinge.

Part II – POLITICS

4 Democracy Celebrated

A Swiss-Swedish political scientist and global democracy reporter, Bruno Kaufmann, visits Denmark's biggest political festival in Allinge on Bornholm. Folkemødet (The People's Meeting) has been held annually in Allinge since 2011.

By Bruno Kaufmann

"*Tak for det*, thank you, Gunnar!" These words quickly cross my mind, this bright night on my long march through a barley field. Gunnar *had* warned me in a message earlier that day: "Our black German Shepherd dog will probably meet you halfway…". And *yes,* he did, in a very impressive way. He started barking from afar, and ran towards me at great speed.

In any similar situation, I would have turned back long ago. But now, after a whole day of traveling towards Denmark's most remote island, in the heart of the southern Baltic Sea, I just wanted to go to bed. Probably the last bed available on Bornholm in mid-June, when a whole country turns its gaze eastward.

And I didn't just receive a warning from my host – a farmer I never met during my three-day stay on the island. Gunnar, who owns Kofoed Ringebygård, an impressive farm near the village of Vestermarie on Bornholm, also gave me the code word which turned me from foe to friend, in the eyes of the impressive Alsatian. Its name: Cuba!

My first meeting with Cuba

So, these became my first words on the island: "*Godaften Cuba, kan du tage mig med til mit værelse?*" (Good evening, Cuba, can you please show me to my room?) This was an immediate success, kind of a preview of my forthcoming days here, which would all be about dialogues and meetings, impressions and expressions. I arrived on Bornholm on the eve of *Folkemødet,* The People's Meeting.

For three days every year in mid-June, the sleepy harbour village of Allinge-Sandvig, with a population of just under 1,500 people, transforms into a democratic powerhouse, a meeting place of tens of thousands of active citizens, leading politicians, energized businesspeople, and slick lobbyists. This is a festival, under the Nordic midsummer sun, of a very special kind, in a unique place on earth.

I'll get back to that in just a moment.

However, lying down in my comfy bed, that warm night on Gunnar's farm, my thoughts went back to Gotland, another Baltic island, where – more than 30 years earlier – I had for the first time experienced a "democracy festival", as *Folkemødet* calls itself today: Gotland, around 350 kilometers to the north, is Bornholm's much bigger sister, with an area of more than 3,184 km² (Bornholm: 588 km²), and a population of 61,000 (Bornholm: 40,000).

The vanguard aircraft carriers

Historically and geopolitically a kind of fixed, vanguard aircraft carrier facing Russia in times of crisis, both Gotland and Bornholm became holiday destinations of choice for the fashionable set of both Sweden and

Denmark, during the second half of the 20th century. In the late 1960s, Olof Palme, a leading Swedish Social Democratic politician, had the brilliant idea of combining his summer holiday with a political appearance.

Palme, who later became Prime Minister, and in 1986 was tragically murdered by a man still unknown to this day, travelled once every summer from his cottage in the north of Gotland to Almedalen Park, in the heart of the island capital, Visby. Here, he used the back of a truck and a megaphone to share his thoughts with other holidaymakers. He and the audience liked this unusual format, and they came back every summer, in growing numbers.

By 1991, when I reported from Almedalen Week for the first time – the name of the place had become the name of the democracy festival – the Social Democratic Party event had turned into an all-party, open-air meeting engaging locals and visitors alike over several days. It also attracted more and more foreign guests, such as leading politicians from both Bornholm and Copenhagen, which led to the establishment of *Folkemødet* in Allinge-Sandvig, 20 years later.

A paternalistic show turns participatory

So, another twelve years later, I'm on my way to *Folkemødet* again. As a reporter for the Swiss Broadcasting Corporation, covering Northern European Affairs and democracy developments around the world, I have followed the developments of these new forms of practising and celebrating active citizenship and assembly democracy with great interest over the years, experiencing the metamorphosis of the rather top-down, paternalistic features of representative democracy into much more grassroots, participatory ways of agenda-setting and decision-making.

My first decision on that first day of yet another *Folkemøde* is personal: how to get to the heart of the action in Bornholm's northeast. I choose Bus #1, which links the quiet village of Vestermarie with Allinge-Sandvig, whose narrow streets are already bustling before midday. Along as many as 40 stops, the bus picks up other attendees who have found somewhere on the island a place for a last quiet night of sleep.

Because during *Folkemødet,* there will be very little of this. "I'm here to party for democracy and peace", says a young Danish woman in wildly colourful clothes, joining the bus halfway up to Allinge. And indeed, *Folkemødet* offers plenty of opportunities not to sleep, as workshops, seminars, and politicians' speeches may turn into dinner roundtables, DJ battles, and psychedelic dance parties, over the course of the short mid-June nights.

The unique Bornholmian way of democratic *hygge*

Folkemødet in Allinge-Sandvig, which has been organized annually since 2011, is not simply a copy-and-paste edition of the "original" democracy festival in Almedalen, on Gotland. It's a unique Danish and Bornholmian way of engaging in political dialogue across the entire ideological spectrum, and is very much rooted in the Danish way of life, also known as *hygge.*

No people celebrates its democracy like the Danes. They are one of the most politically engaged nations: 3.5 million of the country's 4 million eligible voters participated in the last national election in 2022 — a rate of almost 85 percent. By tradition, Danes show their happiness and engagement by waiting for the voting results together, and talking out their differences over beer. The competing political parties gather in the Parliament for Danish "Democracy Night," or *Snapstinget* (literally, "The Brandy Parliament").

British author Helen Russell, who wrote *The Year of Living Danishly: Uncovering the Secrets of the World's Happiest Country*, makes a similar point: "The Danish have a deep contentment with themselves, and with their lives, which creates a solidarity and makes people more trusting of one another, and less stressed." She adds that "happiness in Denmark is seen as a process rather than a permanent state; something that you actively work at every day, by making the most of little things, indulging in pleasure like sex or pastry, working less, and being with your family more."

"Everything Mr Putin has started a war against"

All this and much more can be felt and experienced during the short but intense days of *Folkemødet*. The concept has been so inspiring to visitors from abroad that similar democracy festivals have more recently been established in most countries around the Baltic Sea. It's a part of the world where the great ideas of societies based on peaceful democracy and social justice have come a long way. But it's also a place where the opposite is threateningly noticeable: "*Folkemødet* embodies everything Mr Putin has started a war against," comments the local newspaper, *Bornholms Tidende*.

And as *Folkemødet* evolves over days and nights, with thousands of small and larger events, the first war in Europe since 1945, involving the world's largest country (Russia) against Europe's largest democracy (Ukraine) provides a very serious framework to a very relaxed festival. At one point, Russian warships appear on the horizon, cruising the waters where in 2022, in a foggy, night-time action, still unconfirmed saboteurs destroyed the Russian-German gas pipeline, Nord Stream, a few kilometers beyond the shores of Bornholm.

Heading back to my quiet, cosy bed on Gunnar's farm, on a night bus route basically crisscrossing the whole island, on an early sunny summer's morning, we pass the giant bunkers at Dueodde, in the very south of Bornholm. Here, during the Second World War, Nazi occupiers tried to establish a battery of 380 mm guns, to make the island an impregnable fort. In the end, Soviet bombers ended the German occupation, and themselves tried to stay – until 1946. Even today, Moscow is claiming special rights to Bornholm, making it a very important and delicate place indeed to celebrate the annual democracy festival.

Making the best of difficult times

And while Allinge and Bornholm hit the Danish headlines once a year during *Folkemødet*, the locals don't always feel too good about the concept. There's an obvious flipside to the grand march of politically active citizens from Denmark and beyond. High prices, lots of waste, and drunk participants are just some of the downsides. But as throughout history, which for this beautiful and welcoming island has been a true rollercoaster ride, Bornholm tries not only to adapt, but also to make the best of it.

Including farmer Gunnar and his impressive Alsatian Cuba, who once a year have to deal with curious guests from far afield, like me. *Tak for det!*

Part III – CULTURE

5 Of Trolls and the Underground Landscape

The bus from Copenhagen drops people off at the tourist office in Rønne harbour. It's a convenient place to pick up maps or hiking guides or restaurant listings, before you set off. But wait, you think, as your eyes fall on a children's book available not only in Danish and Bornholmsk, but also in English and German: Who is that little red guy on the cover, and why is he important to Bornholm? Anthropologist Lars Kofoed Rømer sheds light on the island's "Subterraneans" – the rock or burial mound-dwelling creatures familiar to every child on Bornholm, in his PhD dissertation entitled "Tales in an Underground Landscape". Interview by Tina Hirschbuehl.

Interview with Lars Kofoed Rømer

Who is Krølle-Bølle, and why is he so enduringly popular on Bornholm?

Krølle-Bølle is the name of the young troll in a 1946 children's book by Ludvig Mahler. Mahler, who worked for the Bornholm railways, wrote and illustrated it for his son during World War II, and it was subsequently published as a sort of tourist guide. Krølle-Bølle lives with his family in Langebjerg, a hill near Sandvig, in the north of Bornholm, and has a habit of leaving his abode to visit some of the popular attractions on Bornholm, teasing the humans he encounters on his way. If in trouble, Krølle-Bølle invokes the name of his father, Bobbaækus, as a spell to protect him from harm.

The books were hugely popular, and the little troll became the island's tourism mascot, his image found on everything from keychains and mugs to ice cream. In fact, when it was announced that I had been granted funding by the Danish Council for Independent Research for my PhD research on the Subterraneans on Bornholm, it was derided in the Danish media as "Krølle-Bølle research". The international press joined in on the ridicule, reporting that the Danish government had hired a professional troll hunter.

Other academics came to your defence, saying that the project had been misunderstood. It wasn't a tree-hugging project about the supernatural, it was about understanding how people – ordinary people – understand the world. And how they relate to the landscapes they live in.

My idea was to try to approach Bornholm in a similar way to how anthropologists – since the dawn of the discipline – have studied faraway islands and cultures, with a special focus on how storytelling, myths, animism, and magic often play an important part in people's everyday life. But I think that in a Western and European context, there tends to be a common understanding that we have long since abandoned such elements, through the process of rationalization, and the disenchanting effects of modernity. To me, this seemed too simplified – and not really in accordance with how I could see people engage with the landscape on Bornholm, where I was born and raised. The many folk tales I came across while applying to do my PhD also suggested that there might be a different and slightly hidden story to be told – one that offered an alternative understanding of what it means to live on a modern, Western European island.

You completed your PhD, and have since carved out quite a niche for yourself as an expert on this topic, which clearly fascinates people. You're in high demand as a speaker at schools, museums, and events, and you're working on two books on the subject. I'm guessing you weren't literally "hunting trolls", as the press described – so what did you set out to discover?

I studied how the landscape of Bornholm is both living, lived, and lived in – viewing this as an ever-unfolding process that interweaves multiple histories, places, and intimate entanglements between non-human and human agents. I sought to conceptualize the underground qualities of a landscape.

I started by gathering material from the Danish Folklore Archives. Much of it described how, until the recent past, Bornholm was seen as inhabited by patriotic and protective nature beings known in Danish as *de Underjordiske* – which I have translated as "the Subterraneans". I then conducted 10 months of anthropological fieldwork on the island. Drawing on the works of anthropologist Michael Taussig and philosopher Walter Benjamin, I tried to demonstrate how the underground, as an ethnographic trope, aims to capture different elements of Bornholm's landscape, characterized by a movement between concealment and revelation.

The underground landscape is composed of different engagements with the island's bedrock: on the one hand, buried objects from prehistory and Subterranean inhabitants, whether real or imagined; on the other, feelings of terror, neglect, and envy. Social activities such as hunting, walking, metal detecting, storytelling, and memory work can give rise to awe, intimacy, and companionship. Such qualities emerge as the result of different ways of cultivating the landscape. I describe how these cultivations have a tale-like character where historical events or monuments blend with folk legends, and infuse the island with an undercurrent of enchantment that not only brings the landscape to life, but also affects the people who inhabit it. In doing so, I reject a strict separation between factual and made-up history.

You mention that in the Old Norse root of the word landscape – "landskapr" – "skapr" means both a sort of container, and the act of shaping and creating. So landscape isn't something detached from humans – rather, it's shaped by human engagement with the land, and immersion in it. In other words, the people and the landscape co-create each other.

That's right. Bornholm's landscape can be recognized as both lived, and living, through various practices: in hunting, in walking, in looking at old photos in a town's local archive, or in acknowledging the presence of prehistoric monuments. Subterraneans may be present both as stories and in actual experiences, and they can be evoked by scout leaders, tour guides, teachers, amateur archaeologists, or simply as tales passed on from parent to child. I argue that the different ways people on Bornholm relate to a particular place, and are affected by the landscape they inhabit, should be seen as "an ongoing conversation with an animated environment". It's a phrase I've borrowed from Danish anthropologist Kirsten Hastrup, who conducted her research in Iceland, and who was my PhD supervisor.

How did people on the island react when you first started asking questions about the Subterraneans?

At first, the main reaction was that the Subterraneans were something people used to believe in in the olden days, but not any more. Right after telling me this, people often gave a little laugh or smile. In fact, the immediate relegation of the Subterraneans to the past – making it a historical topic – happened so often that it suggested a general, public understanding of how Bornholm's contemporary landscape has been disenchanted.

Are any reasons given as to why the landscape is no longer as enchanted as in the past?

One common idea is that there were two major disenchanters: lighting and cars. Electricity and the light bulb had the effect of illuminating the old superstitions and misconceptions. And the speed of motorized vehicles on paved roads made the landscape less terrifying, when moving through it. Electricity brought light into the once dark, shadowy corners of houses, and compared to following murky paths on foot or horseback, the speed, lights, and metal casing provided by cars on paved country roads undoubtedly created a different sensory experience of the landscape. It made it harder to question straightforward explanations for odd events.

However, new sources of light also create new shadows – and new technologies, such as metal detectors, also create new opportunities for personal engagement with the landscape.

Since the 17th century, a trope of disenchantment and "pastness" has been an integral part of the way that tales of Subterraneans have been recorded and presented. But this may not necessarily be an accurate expression of what's truly going on. I'd argue that such denials can be seen as enacting a form of public secrecy where people know "what not to know", to limit the risk of being punished or ridiculed.

In other words, people are afraid to mention their personal stories related to the Subterraneans, for fear of being mocked?

Something like that, yes. Several people I met mentioned people they knew who had had an experience. For example, Edith, who was 85 when I spoke to her. As a child, Edith's late father had returned home one evening, after dropping off the daily newspaper to his grandfather, and found the yard and shed full of little people – Subterraneans. Too scared to stay, he ran back to his grandfather. Edith said that when she was a child, her father had told her other tales of dangerous beings inhabiting the streams and harbour, but only shared this personal experience when she was over 30. "Nobody has experiences like this any more," says Christina, a guide in Gudhjem, adding that she only knows of two people who say they do. However, she has heard quite a few people talk about how their parents or grandparents really believed, back in the day.

In other cases, people knew of bad things that had happened to those who disrespected Subterranean places, such as burial mounds. One person I spoke to, Torben, pointed out a house that was named after a burial mound. However, the mound had been destroyed by a previous owner, with dire consequences. Torben said he had heard it from Edwin, the owner's son. "There is a saying that if someone disturbs a burial mound, he will be dead before the next midsummer. And that's what happened. Edwin's father died."

What about personal experiences with Subterraneans? Did anyone approach you with those?

Well, sometimes it can be tricky to determine what people have actually experienced. In many cases, an experience that comes from the feeling of an animated landscape is tactile, auditive, or emotional. But I have also been in contact with people who have had distinct visual experiences.

During the first month of the project, I received an e-mail from a young woman, Thea, about a childhood experience she wanted to share. Now in her twenties and studying to be a nurse, Thea recalled how at the age of five, while on holiday, she had been out walking with her father and older brother.

"We were on our way towards Hammershus, in an area with small hills, large stones and bedrock here and there. It was grazing land, but close to a forest. My dad rested on a hill, while my brother and I went looking for trolls. We had heard about Krølle-Bølle and reasoned that there should be trolls somewhere near the forest. We walked separately. I went up a hill where a chunk of rock had formed a cavern, a sort of open shed in the hill, lowered my head to peer into the hollow, and glimpsed a strange being — a little man wearing clothes made of leaves. He had a pointed hat with what I recall as a red band around it. His hat, too, was made of leaves, and green; his nose peeped out below it. I cannot remember seeing his eyes. Under his nose, he had a large, white beard. I was certain he was a

troll, but when I think about it, he looked more like a pixie."

Thea says she did not get to study him any closer, since the sight gave her such a shock that she immediately withdrew her head and ran crying to her father, and refused to be left alone for the rest of the holiday. In late June 2016, I visited the area with Thea and her fiancé, and as we walked around looking for the particular rock formation, she recalled hearing many stories about various nature-beings during her childhood. The well-known Danish children's books about the little troll Troldepus who, similarly to Krølle-Bølle, lived in a mound with his family, and ventured out into the world of humans, were frequently read aloud to her, and when out walking in the forests, every now and then, someone would tell a short troll tale. Both her mother and aunt were open to the existence of such beings, and at times, Thea would play in the woods with her brother and cousins, while her aunt would act as *lygtemand* – "lantern man" – a small being mentioned in stories who used a lantern to try to lure people into the marshes.

Following a line of reasoning by the late anthropologist Margaret Mead, Thea can be seen as being educated in animism from an early age. She remembers how the troll tales and games ignited a sense of adventure about the forests, as well as the wonder of nature in general. Reflecting further on the experience, Thea recalls a few other "illusions" she had as a child, which she believes were caused by fatigue or rapid movements causing objects around her to become distorted, and take on a different appearance. Regarding the green-leafed pixie, she reasoned that since she was out looking for trolls, this might have created a "dream image" in the hollow space of the hill. But she didn't feel that this reasoning added up, in the specific experience she remembers. There was no object in the hollow space that could be distorted, and if the vision was her own mental projection created by the stories she had been told, why did it take the appearance of a strange little forest pixie, and not the trolls she had heard about?

Do you have other examples of contemporary personal experiences of the Subterraneans?

Yes, I can tell you about Viola. The first time she told me the story, when I visited her in her apartment in Nexø, Viola paused, and nervously asked if I had heard about others with similar experiences. When I confirmed that there are indeed similar accounts in the archival records, Viola breathed a sigh of relief. "Then I'm not the only one!"

Together, we drove to the area around the church in Poulsker. We pull over, she shakes her body, then looks, and points down the road toward the small house that was her childhood home: "It's not a good place." It was between those two roadside trees, still standing, now much taller, that she was once out picking wild strawberries. It was summer, and the sun was high, when she suddenly heard music: trumpets, drums, and a kind of flute. She can't remember the melody, but it was certainly not jazz (which she likes). She stood up and saw a small orchestra, with the leader, somewhat larger than the others, wearing a pointed red hat and red cape. They were walking on the road towards the Ringelhøj burial mound. Viola reasoned that they were either coming from the hill at Præstehøjen, the Priest's Mound, right next to the church, and were on their way to visit their relatives in Ringelhøj, or they came from Ringelhøj, and were on their way back, after visiting Præstehøj. While the vision, as she recalls, was more surprising than scary, she didn't dare tell her parents, who were working on the other side of the road. Their relationship was not close, and she often felt alone and excluded, which she later attributed to the fact that, as she learned as a teen, they were her adoptive parents. "You think you're crazy when you see something like this," she notes, and she didn't want her parents to exclude her even more.

In a small segment of a local radio show broadcast a few years ago, Viola heard an elderly man tell a similar story of hearing the Subterraneans play, but couldn't recall hearing such stories when she was a child. While we might speculate whether the absence of Subterranean tales in Viola's childhood was due to public secrecy or disinterest, her vision bears a strong resemblance to tales kept in the folklore archive, as well as a few reprinted legends. Several of the recorded tales from before Viola was born tell of people either seeing or hearing the Subterraneans playing drums and fifes during their military drills, or music and light emanating from the burial mounds during Subterranean parties. In fact, some of the tales are recorded as taking place in the very same area where Viola lived.

Telling fairy stories to children is common to many cultures. To what extent is passing on stories about the Subterraneans a form of cultural education?

To a very high extent. Arguably one of the most prominent writers of modern fairy tales, JRR Tolkien, noted in 1939 that associating children and fairy stories is an accident of our domestic history — that, in the "modern lettered world", as he calls it, such stories have been relegated to the nursery. But rather than understanding this as adult disinterest, it may also be seen as a way of locating beliefs in the distant past or a distant place, such as Iceland, creating a licensed narrative space for talking about an enchanted landscape. And making myths and legends a natural element of childhood can, in turn, be a way for adults to carry their culture forward.

The teachers I talked to on Bornholm were well aware that telling such stories to children was a form of cultural education. On the one hand, it was a way of passing on a sense of respect towards the natural surroundings, and raising the children's awareness of its history. On the other, telling such tales was simply seen as a way of continuing the tradition of local storytelling, which they considered an important aspect of living on the island.

Growing up in the 1940s, my mother recalls a sense of mystique related to certain areas or weather phenomena on the island. For example, every time they passed Langebjerg, her father always pointed it out as the dwelling place of the Subterraneans. When out gathering mushrooms, those growing in a circular formation would be a "Heksering", which translates literally as "witches' ring", but in fact has an English equivalent in the term "fairy ring". And when the white mist created undulating shapes on their frequent journey between Hasle and Rønne, she and her sister were told that the "woman of the marshes was brewing" ("Mosekonen brygger") or that the "the elf girls are dancing" ("Elverpigerne danser"). How common is it for children to grow up with this kind of imagery on the island – and does it serve a purpose?

I heard several accounts during my fieldwork of how school or kindergarten teachers told such tales to children. For example, the mother of a child in the same class as my daughter mentioned during a school party how, a few months after she and her family moved to Bornholm, their youngest daughter had been told in kindergarten that Subterraneans lived in burial mounds, and she was now scared to pass the mound close to their home.

The tales of different beings inhabiting particular places in Bornholm's landscape may also be seen as a spatial prohibition that infuses places with fear – be they wells, moors, streams, or the sea. For instance, Smil, a man in his nineties from Svaneke, who passed away in 2023, explained that children were told to avoid the sea when *havkjættan* appeared in the white waves – in other words, when the surf was wild. Smil noted how the tales had worked as "nannies" at a time when children were left much to themselves. Populating childhood landscapes with nature beings such as *kjætter* (female cat) and *bobber* (ghost, troll, or bogeyman) can thus be a way of instilling in children a touch of vigilance and fear about places that might be dangerous for them.

But it wasn't just a way of instilling fear, was it? What about positive experiences?

Telling children such stories can also be a way of fostering respect for the history and cultural value of places. On one occasion, I accompanied a troop of Scouts to a boulder near Nexø known as the Devil's Bowling Alley (*Fandens Keglebane*). The boulder's name referred to the numerous Bronze Age cupmarks engraved in its surface, which were believed to be finger imprints of the devil who threw the rock. Another name for the same boulder is Money Stone (*Pengestenen*), due to the coins that have allegedly been found in the cupmarks at times. In a ceremony that involved an atmospheric walk in the forest, the children placed knives they had carved out of wood into the cupmarks on the boulder, as gifts to the Subterraneans. Shortly afterwards, they were rewarded with a find of chocolate coins. This activity was not intended as a way to instil fear and deterrence. Rather, as a ceremonial act, it demonstrated a seriousness about how people should interact with tales about the Subterraneans.

As Scout leader Lena later noted, the point of the activity was not so much to make the children believe in Subterraneans, or suggest that they actually lived under the boulder. Rather, it was a way to transmit a message. As a narrative form, tales have long been seen as a useful way to communicate with children. So, while invoking Subterraneans as mound and rock dwellers might frighten some of the children, what was more important was fostering respect for both the cultural value of these places, and for the landscape and the island's history in general. While the beings' potency as bearers of culture would probably diminish as the children got older, the idea here is that childhood memories of a ceremony such as the one at the Money Stone would ensure that a touch of this knowledge and respect would hopefully stay with them.

What's in play here is an understanding of childhood as a prolonged, loosely defined temporal space where spirits of nature can legitimately be invoked as real presences serving a pedagogical aim, as children are more receptive to these kinds of narratives.

Presumably, stories people have heard as a child are often passed on to their own children, and become family tales?

Absolutely. This became clear during several conversations I had – how places become a part of what constitutes a family, and how visiting or carrying out a ritual at such a place becomes a way of welcoming new members, such as a daughter-in-law or a son-in-law, into a family. This was the case for Kirsten's family.

Kirsten had always told her grandchildren about a place called Varparna, a group of three stone beacons in the inland plantation of Pedersker parish. On Bornholm, this kind of beacon is known as a *pilt*, which in Old Norse means "little boy". This particular pilt, however, doesn't relate to the death of a young boy, but to the tragic story of how three sisters were killed along with their coachman while on their way to matins at Østermarie church. There are various versions of the tale, but in all of them, the perpetrators were the three brothers of the young women, who had been sent away by the parents, to prevent the fulfilment of a witch's prophecy that they would kill their siblings.

Whenever Kirsten's grandchildren visited, they would insist on going to Varparna with Kirsten, so she could retell the story, and they could place a flower or a stone on the pilts. "This is what you do to show respect," Kirsten said, as she had heard from many people on the island. As well as passing on this sense of respect and enacting it herself, what emerged from Kirsten's account was how doing so had also become part of what constituted their family. On a recent visit, for instance, the granddaughter had brought along her new boyfriend, and insisted that they all visit Varparna, so that the boyfriend could hear Kirsten tell the story. As Kirsten recalled, it felt like a way to begin making him part of the family. This brings to mind other anthropological studies – such as one done in Chile by Alberto Jímenez Corsin in 2003 – in which particular places, like playgrounds or a shopping mall, are seen not just as geographical locations, but as vehicles for the expression of social relationships. Similarly, Varparna wasn't just a backdrop for Kirsten's family relations, but a vehicle for the way they became and acted as a family.

As another example of how a particular place becomes part of a particular family's way of being, Andreas, the husband of one of my anthropological colleagues, shared his recollection of how, when driving on a particular road on Bornholm, his father would always tell the same story. It was on the way to the family's summer house, and sitting with his younger brother in the back seat, the boys would look at each other with excitement, as they approached the church in Poulsker.

According to the tale told by his father – who I later learnt had heard the story from *his* father, a country doctor, when he was out visiting patients – builders had begun constructing the church on top of the hill called the Priest's Mound, *Præstehøjen*. You'll recall that it was also from here that Viola had seen a band of Subterraneans march with drums and fifes down the road to the next mound. But as Andreas shared, his father would describe how everything built by the humans during the day was demolished by the Subterraneans during the night. But when the human workers gave up on the site and began building just a short distance from the mound, whatever they erected by day was doubled by night.

Andreas recalled that he and his brother would giggle at the thought of the Subterraneans teasing the humans, and share the feeling that the humans had it coming, since they were the ones disturbing the Subterraneans' home. Again, an element of showing respect towards one's surroundings is certainly present here, but what is perhaps more important is how the Priest's Mound, as well as the process of approaching it, driving past, and leaving it behind, is incorporated into the sense of family that has been passed on from Andreas's grandfather to his father, and which he now, after recently becoming a father himself, looks forward to passing on to his daughter.

Let's turn to walking – which, after all, is one of the activities that attracts visitors to the island. Even on relatively short walks, you're spoilt for fantastic views and great variety in the landscape. Will walkers visiting Bornholm be able to sense the Subterranean presence?

Everybody here seems to walk all the time, with all sorts of intentions, temperaments, and purposes. There are solitary walks, therapeutic walks, dog-walking, sports or exercise walks, social walks, walking groups, themed walks, or walks with a specific goal: to hunt, to search for prehistoric artefacts, or to pick mushrooms.

Communal walks can be a way of exploring and attuning yourself and others to a more general sense of how Bornholm's landscape is defined by multiplicity. An outing like this can be seen as offering a continuing sense of ownership of the landscape, connecting some of the educational elements I've mentioned, such as tales told to children. Another aspect might be the advancement of hunting ethics, where the sharp separation between nature and humans is broken down. These kinds of outing highlight the uniqueness of any experience in moving through a landscape, as it is always shifting, creating a myriad of different places, people, times, and seasons. Geographer Sarah Whatmore coined the term "hybrid geographies" to describe the world as a combination of heterogeneous social encounters, with "bonds" between – her words – people and plants, devices and creatures, documents, and elements.

As part of my field research, I joined a group of 40 senior citizens who meet year-round every Tuesday to go walking. During a three-hour walk and picnic in the Paradise Hills in early May 2016, a wide range of conversation topics, tales, subtle sensations, objects shaped by human hands, and elements of nature moved in and out of our presence. During this walk, as a way to explain what was special about Bornholm, Kristoffer brought up the tale of how God, after creating the world, was left with a handful of the best elements. Hurling the forests, rocks, and beaches held in his hand into the Baltic, he created Bornholm.

Many cultures have their fairies, elves, gnomes, and other animist creatures. The Nordic countries have long been associated with "trolls", depicted in various forms. It seems to be very much part of the fabric of Bornholm, too. Even a recent play at Rønne Theatre – Sne (Snow) – addressed the issue, and this was a play for adults, not a fairy tale for children. Is Bornholm a particular hotspot for Subterraneans – and what makes it so?

Well, we need to make a distinction between the term "troll" and the Subterraneans. In a Bornholm context, trolls are large creatures who predominantly live not on Bornholm, but in southern Sweden, from where they throw large boulders at the churches on Bornholm, because they hate the sound of church bells. While trolls can easily be distinguished from humans, Subterraneans are distinctly human-like, and although they may appear in different sizes and clothing, they almost always mirror the human inhabitants of the landscape.

In terms of prevalence on Bornholm, in the Danish Folklore Archives, Bornholm is certainly not the place with the most tales. But my research showed that the Subterraneans and the sentiments they capture are still very much part of the present landscape on Bornholm. I haven't studied other parts of Denmark, so I'm not sure about the current state of contemporary enchantment elsewhere.

Part of the reason why the stories are still relevant on Bornholm is that many of them are connected to either the archaeological or the military history of the island. The stories about the Subterranean army that defends Bornholm – and ensured that Bornholm belonged to Denmark – captures a key sentiment of how the island is perhaps "not quite Danish", and often has to fend for itself, or is at risk of being neglected by the nation, when it comes to dealing with foreign enemies. Similarly, while many burial mounds have been destroyed in recent centuries, part of the reason why so many can still be seen in the landscape, as small islands of history floating in the cultivated fields, can perhaps be attributed to the many stories of how you might be punished, if you mess with the homes of the Subterranean dwellers.

You've told us about Varparna. Can you give us other examples of monuments on Bornholm that still inspire awe and reactions in local people?

Well, there's "Holy Woman", the stone megaliths that to this day, people greet when they pass. Tall and slender, Holy Woman is, as she must have been for millennia, hard to miss, for anybody taking the coastal road between Gudhjem and Svaneke. Holy Woman is located on the north-eastern shore of the island, between the old fishing hamlets of Bølshavn and Listed, and consists of one large upright and one fallen Bronze Age megalith on a low mound, with another small boat-shaped circle of stones from the later Iron Age a few metres away.

One tale describes Holy Woman as a memorial stone under which a mother is buried with her ten children, who were killed by their father. Another tells of how the woman petrified herself and her children to protect them, turning them into the megaliths we still greet today. My fieldwork confirmed that the gesture of raising one's hand and saying "Hello Holy Woman" was not just a historical practice, but also very much connected to the present landscape. As Henrik, a retired ambulance driver, explained, it was something he had done since he was a child, and throughout his 40 years on the job. Similarly, many others related how the practice of greeting Holy Woman was something that ran in their respective families. And the husband of one of my wife's friends related how, shortly after moving to Bornholm a few years back, he took a taxi from Listed to Allinge and during the journey, the driver said you should always remember to greet Holy Woman when passing. Whereas tales about Subterraneans were shrouded in denial and secrecy, especially in relation to outsiders, these kinds of tales seemed more readily shared.

One of the recurring themes on Bornholm is the end of World War II, and how the islanders felt abandoned when the rest of Denmark was celebrating the end of the war in early May 1945, while Russian bombs were falling on Rønne and Nexø. A sizeable force of Russian troops stayed on the island until 6 April 1946 – a full 11 months after the end of the war. This topic has even found its way into your PhD. Can you explain?

It's really a recurring topic of conversation here – and yes, it was even relevant to my study. How, for example, the Russian presence can still be felt in town in a phantomic kind of way, despite few traces remaining from the actual 11-month Russian presence in 1945–46. And how the destroyed houses – quickly replaced after the bombings by the "Swedish houses", which are very visible reminders in the townscape today – came to stand as symbols of Danish absence and neglect. These issues emerged from discussions among a group of people who meet weekly at the Nexø Archives to view old photographs together, on a large screen. Many of the photos show their town smashed to pieces. Group members talked about where the precise impact points of the bombs were, the degree to which this had affected different houses, how the cleaning of the town had been organized, and so forth. Rather than fear, the photo discussions most often provoked a sense of how Bornholm, from the May 1945 bombings onwards – indeed to this day – had been somewhat abandoned by Denmark. As an instance of what social anthropologist Yael Navaro-Yashin calls a "phantomic presence", a Russian ghost haunts the streets of Nexø, between the old half-timbered houses, and the many new brick buildings constructed after the war. The same is the case in Rønne, where memorial reliefs commemorate the event on the facades of houses. One reads: "1945. This house remained standing". The Swedish houses, built as replacement homes to those destroyed by the bombs, also carry some of the previous Russian presence. Similarly, the present-day sound of fighter jets frequently heard around the coast also has this phantomic presence. Although the planes are Danish, they are often in the air to ward off Russian planes getting too close to Danish airspace, which ends off the coast of Bornholm. This has increased in the last few years, and to several of the old Bornholmers, it is somewhat reminiscent of the sounds of 1945, a time when many islanders felt a general sense of neglect.

Now, the continuing insistence on the need for such recognition may appear rather counterintuitive, through the lens of Bornholm's growing popularity as a tourist destination for many Danes. You could even say Bornholm occupies a key political position in Denmark, as host of June's annual People's Meeting for more than a decade now. Yet through the lens of many people on Bornholm seeing or experiencing the island's terrain, in both in a historical and contemporary context, as infused with a higher or lesser degree of terror, it is perhaps less surprising. While the imminence of international terror appears to be increasing every day, even on a small island such as Bornholm, there is also the presence of a local sense of ongoing neglect. Whereas for some, the roars of fighter jets in the skies evoke a historical shiver akin to what Taussig calls "terror as usual", there is also a related sense of what might be called "neglect as usual", caused by a perceived historical absence of the "Fatherland", and intimately linked to the island's geographical location not in an insert on the map, but at the easternmost edge of the kingdom.

Lars Christian Kofoed Rømer's PhD dissertation, *Tales in an Underground Landscape*, is available as an e-book.

6 The Living Landscape

Dennis Gade Kofod is an established Danish author of several novels, many of which take place on Bornholm, where he grew up. In "Det levende land" (The Living Landscape), Dennis Gade Kofod retells folktales from the island. Some of these tales are printed here, for the first time in translation.

By Dennis Gade Kofod

I've tried to imagine how the legends might have sounded before they were hastily collected and written down. This is, of course, a vain and false approach, but I don't see my work with the Bornholm treasure trove of stories as archaeological, or archival. Not at all. Instead, I see myself as a new link in the chain of storytellers who help to keep alive the landscape, and all the fantastic beings that inhabit it. It's also where I believe I can contribute to our common understanding of this part of Denmark: in rewriting, in retelling.

For me, these tales are not just good stories. For me, they are invocations that bring the landscape to life. Breathing life and soul into it, so that it's no longer under our full control. For me, the legends – reading them to others or recounting them – is a ritual invoking a magic that spreads from teller to listeners, and from there into what we call reality. A magic that challenges our senses and our propensity for logic, thus forcing us to contemplate our own life, and what gives it value. A ritual and magic that removes humankind from the centre of the universe, because we understand that there are forces at play more powerful than us. As for facts and the basis for the legends – where this runs counter to our knowledge today, I have chosen to trust the tales.

***

The stones have a life, and that's why they are given a name. That's how most of Bornholm is named, and those who know the names of things have a special power over places, and can feel more confident walking around the landscape. Say a nice hello to the world that holds your body inside it is a simple rule of life that gives you reason to look after the world we share. This has only struck me in the last few years, but my initiation into the various names began as early as I can remember. *Hundsemyre* and *Mosekonen*, *Melåen* and *Åbobban*. Then further from the area around Balka. My father always greets Holy Woman and her children. So do I. She and her children are at Bølshavn. Once, they were all living people, but when an evil troll from inside the island threatened the woman and her children, she who was wise to the point of being magical turned them and herself to stone, to hide till better times.

So much knowledge hidden right there, about being a family and loving each other.

Hiding in the landscape like that.

I always think of my own children, when I see her with hers. I wonder when they'll feel safe enough to come back to life? What does she think of the world she looks out onto? Is it not good enough?

Here are some more examples:

Løvehovederne, the Lion Heads, rise out of the sea at *Hammershus*. They are named after what they resemble.

Near one of the heads, the island opens up in a small crevice called *Gåserenden*, the Goose Groove, which goes underground and flows out into the sea again at *Sorte Gryde*, the Black Cauldron. It is named after the two geese that once swam through there so beautifully to fatten themselves on the green grass on the rocks, but which, upon wanting to return to the Lion Heads, had become so fat that they got stuck, and in time, turned into the two round, white stones that can be seen today. Others say that Goose Groove ends at Jons Kapel, where there is a place bearing the same name.

The Lion Heads are not to be confused with *Kamelhovederne*, the Camel Heads.

Studene (which translates as "stud", as in cattle) are two ferocious rocky skerries south of the beautiful harbour at Hammerhavn. Like so many other stones, they were thrown by jealous Swedish troll hags who, for some reason or other, wanted to harm the island. Many say the beauty of the island made the hags angry. Considering how hideous they are, that's quite understandable.

Faces like dried-up bogs.

Near Sandvig, there is a small cove called "Grethe Hellie's Harbour". It's named after Grethe, who as a result of a curse that had taken her husband from her, drowned herself and her three children in the sea. She couldn't provide enough food for them, and had to give up.

She told them they were going fishing, and then pushed the two little boys in. There, right by the shore, the water is deep. The eldest, a girl, was frightened out of her wits, and Grethe tied herself to her, so that they drowned together.

People who committed suicide were not buried in consecrated ground, so her body was buried where Hotel Nordlandet now stands. As if in mockery, it was once called Hotel Romantik.

Now the place is called *Korsbjerg*, or "Cross Mountain", because someone was human enough, after all, to put up a cross for Grethe.

Every eve of the Feast of the Annunciation, a soft, warm light burns over *Fandens keglebane*, the Devil's Bowling Alley, near Nexø. And the holes in the stone are said to have been poked by the hand of the Devil himself. As a child, I never dared cycle that way after tennis, unless I had someone to go with.

The "Sling Stone" at Gamleborg was thrown at St. Bodil's Church. It was thrown by a witch in Sweden who couldn't stand the sound of the priest's voice. From her garters, she made a sling, and got good speed in the stone that way, but before she could let go, the fabric gave way. It was worn out, because she hadn't taken them off since she got them, when she moved away from home. That's why the stone didn't fly straight, or far enough, and landed where it is today. It bears clear traces of the garters that have eaten into it.

In Højlyngen stands Sortebjerg, and on Sortebjerg stands *Troldeegen*, the Trolls' Oak. Through it, you can crawl down to the realm of the *underjordiske*, the "underearthlings".

An old woman recounts how, as a child, she lost her friend, when his childish spirit took him too close to the tree.

She recounts how he was there so clearly, in his winter clothes, with a blue hat covering his ears. A jumble of movement and colours in the snow-covered landscape. The next moment, he was gone.

***

On a farm in Nylars, the farmer was ever so modern, but many could have told him he was going too far, when he took earth from the mound, to fill the foundations of his new cowshed. He even used the phrase "*to future-proof*". That's what he wanted. Like everyone else, he wished to prepare himself for the misfortunes we always think are coming.

He didn't want to listen to those old people and hags who, according to him, were the only ones who still believed in those… what do you call them? oh so dangerous underearthlings. Such a load of troll stuff is no match for reinforced walls and modern machinery.

Never was there so much disease and unrest in a single stable.

Every night, at least one cow broke loose, and beat itself bloody against the hard new walls.
Boils and mange leapt from heifer to heifer, and none of the vets on the island could stop it.

Calves fell limp and lifeless, like dropped wet sacks of grain.

In the end, the farmer had to give up, to avoid going bankrupt.

With machines just as big as the ones they had built with, they had to break up the concrete, and drive the earth back to where they had taken it.

But he still went bankrupt, in the end. And the farm has not yet been sold.

It's not even that long ago.

∗∗∗

Of the legends I heard more recently, this is the one I like best. It's the way the dream – which of course is itself a story – intervenes in reality, and changes it, because the dreamer chooses to believe what he hears in the dream. That relationship with the story, where you choose to believe, is the seed of my love of stories and of literature

– the way that they can magically change our world. I believe that the experiences we have in stories are just as important as those we have in reality, and that in that way, the stories and what they tell us are true. It's just a question of which world we choose to inhabit.

Per woke up drenched in sweat, but didn't take the time to wash before packing. He had to get to Sweden as fast as possible. In the dream, Per had been promised happiness and wealth once he got there, and so with nothing but a small backpack, he took the boat the same day.

In the dream, Per had been in the city of Karlskrona, but when he arrived there, he couldn't find his way around after all, and ended up having to rent a room. There, as fate would have it, he had to share a bed with another Bornholmer, and Per told him about the dream and his journey. The Bornholmer laughed at him; what idiot follows a whim of the night like that? He himself had once had a dream about an enormous treasure at Hakkeled, and of course he hadn't just left his safe life here in Sweden, where he was married, and made a living as a travelling salesman.

The next day, Per-who-followed-his-dreams travelled back to the island where it had all begun. At Hakkeled, he found the treasure, and with it, was able to buy a farm and labourers, and easily travel wherever he wanted.

***

It's said about the rebellion of 1658 that at the smithy, they put all their silver buttons on the table to be melted into bullets. Everyone knew that the Commander was in league with evil, so ordinary bullets wouldn't hurt him.

That night, they were going to capture Printzensköld, and take the island back for themselves and the King they thought was theirs.

The Danish King.

The mould kept filling with hot metal, and at last they

113

had enough for everyone to defend themselves, should it come to a fight. Already, Villum was nervous – the man who later learns that the bullets work, when he shoots the devil from Skåne who had besmirched the island.

Out on Blemmelyng stands the stone Printzensköld's wife threw in anger, when she heard that the man she had helped with her magic had been shot by simple islanders. Once, it is said, it was possible to see a crater in the landscape, but today it has disappeared. Nevertheless, the stone is so large that it's easy to understand how powerful and strong a witch she was.

And accounts by several of the 120 men the Swedes had on the island tell of how they could feel the rock and the ground under their boots turn against them, until they were on the ship and sailed away from the possessed land. Some of them recount that a heat rose from the ground that could be felt all the way up to the knees, and that the heat did not come from any fire, but felt more like the anger of a parent.

The whole time, the underearthlings were ready to intervene, if the Bornholmers themselves didn't manage to get the Swede thrown off the island.

***

Once, the farm bailiff from Lensberg farm went for an evening walk with his son. They walked to help the digestion of the father, who suffered from slow bowels; or so the doctor made him believe. Everything he ate sat in him for a long time, like a foreign body.

Like a stone in a freshly sown field.

Like a clod of earth on the lawn of the ornamental garden.

The boy kicked at a small round piece of wood that appeared on the path, in front of him. When the father found the energy, he kicked too, and in this way, time passed by itself, as darkness crept in. As the two then got close to the beach, where they wanted to dip their feet in the cold, springtime water, a light shone across the dark landscape. The light, which came from nowhere, but was just there, revealed a group of small underearthling children playing a game that was probably like our kick-the-can. In and out of the landscape went the little bodies. In and out of the light ran the little shadows. As if the number of creatures was constantly doubling and halving. As if they could be in several places at once.

Then the children spotted the two people watching them, and called the bailiff's son, with their bright, clear children's voices that cut through the gathering night, and he at once wanted to go off and play with them. His father, weakened by his illness and in spite of pains in his stomach, only just succeeded in holding him back, until after a while, the light disappeared into itself, and darkness came, so completely and kindly. The boy's clothes were wrinkled and dirty with sweat and earth. He had spit and snot around his mouth. After that, he was never allowed to go out alone, and as an adult, he was gripped by fear that he was chosen to be taken. That's why he always carried steel in both pockets.

***

The girl's two aunts once had to fetch water for their mother when they were big children. This was while the family still lived at Tengselhøj. Together, they walked with the empty bucket dangling between them. The morning dew – for it was summer – gathered around their bare ankles, and tickled their bare feet.

Then, halfway to the well, a little man came up to them. He bowed and, without saying anything, offered them something delicious from a black plate. Sugar balls of some kind that glistened in the sun.

The youngest girl wanted to eat, but the eldest forbade her. And when the man could not make them eat, he asked if they'd go with him to the mound, to get their water there. It would save them part of the way.

Again, the youngest was willing, and her sister had to hold her, for the little man had already taken her by the hand. Like that they stood and pulled, until suddenly, he disappeared.

***

What I write is connected to all the stories I have read and heard. Writing is as much about listening as it is about telling. That says something about the importance of these legends. They are both a link between us and the land we live on, and a link between who we are and who we once were. The more stories you have listened to, the more you have the world in you.

***

A 14-year-old boy was sent from Svaneke to Nexø one winter, so it was dark before he could get home again. First, he had to get past Kurehøj, where the underearthlings were calling him, but he was strong. Then came the stretch of coast with the ghosts of the drowned sailors that the *Malkværn* reef had taken. And again after that, the hill at Årsdale, with the mad woman in the little house, who he knew had chased another boy with a bread knife.

But it all went well.

His steps were the only sound in the night.

Occasionally he saw lights, but convinced himself they were farms where the people sat busying themselves.

Eventually he came to Hesteklewa, where the Hel Horse lived. He shuddered, and tip-toed so as not to make more noise than absolutely necessary. His legs were burning, and he was out of breath from holding his breath, but at last, he was past it, and there would be no further danger till he was home. With the calm came the cold, and he slapped his arms around himself to get warm. The loud slaps echoed, and when the noise had settled, he heard horse's hooves behind him. Without a backward glance, he ran. He kept running, but the whole time, the horse was right behind him. Sweat soaked his woollen cap, and ran into his eyes. The first lights from the town danced here and there. He realized it was the mill.

Then he fell, and had no choice but to wait for death.

He lay there, and could hear the Hel Horse approaching. That's all that happened.

When he got up again, he saw it was only a mare from one of the farms that had followed him.

***

Many of my friends moved to the countryside, when they returned to Bornholm, driven by a dream of freedom that I don't possess. They tease me – affectionately – that I live in a provincial backwater, and I laugh with them. But I love Rønne, which I still – now in my 13th year of living there – don't fully know. Again and again, it's as if the town opens new parts of itself for me, as if I'm only slowly making myself worthy of knowing its secrets.

Yet another plaque commemorating the bombing.

A window that's crooked and has had to be hand-made, because the house was damaged when the Russians attacked.

A murderer's house. Another one.

The ghost at Strien.

The ghost of the old prison where the cobbler hanged himself. It's always with a special pleasure that I read stories from here.

The town isn't all 24-hour petrol stations, and boy racer cars.

The town also has its ghosts and troll hags.

***

My wife works in Rønne, in a kindergarten that used to be a children's home. It was founded in 1843, bombed by the Russians, and rebuilt in 1946. Of course it is haunted,

117

and eventually the complaints from parents and staff were so numerous that the board had the management bring in a wise woman, who called herself a clairvoyant.

Together, they walked slowly through the many small rooms, which are not really suitable for day care at all, but which are actually the key to the cosiness so many people associate with the place. The whole time, the wise woman recounted what she was seeing. A small child, a soldier from the war, an old man who had lost his way, but no ghosts that wanted to harm people. That is, until they're back in the hallway that divides the nursery and kindergarten, where there's always a draught. There, she found a woman who couldn't find peace, but who wouldn't say why. The woman took her anger out on the parents who had come in to drop off their children. On their way out, she whispered a guilty conscience into their ears.

The wise woman lit a St Michael's candle, to give the ghosts peace. That ought to help, and there has been no talk of hauntings since.

***

Only one girl from the class lives in the countryside. All the other pupils live in town. They're playing together when I arrive at the birthday party. It's a large garden that ends at the edge of a forest. Just a few metres into the woods, there's a small mound in a clearing. I've had a cup of coffee and a piece of sweet Danish pastry from the traditional *kagedame* "pastry-woman" birthday cake. The ritual consumption of the birthday child.

I wait for the game to peter out, so that I can allow myself to take my child home. I spend the time walking around the mound, which has a beautiful steep rise. The sun shines on the long grass, and I sit there and eat.

Then more parents arrive, and the party breaks up. The children lose their energy, and want to go home. Their way of saying good-bye is awkward and shy.

As we back out of the courtyard and turn the car around, the kid tells me that they weren't allowed to play on the mound. The father had said so, in the voice that adults use when children are in danger.

I'm pleased all the way back to Rønne.

***

A tourist at the hotel where I grew up nearly drowned in the bay where we went bathing. The sea is usually so calm there, and his parents said he was a good and confident swimmer. A few days later, on the swings in the playground, under the big pine tree, he told me he had felt hands in the water. Not big strong hands like those of an adult, but infinite tiny ones that clung to him, like sand on a damp foot.

I didn't tell him, but I had had the same experience myself, but without feeling it was dangerous. That experience of the sea taking hold of you, and squeezing.

In fact, that experience of the landscape coming alive is one I often have. Often, I find that I am being welcomed in places I go. Alone, or together with my children. That feeling of the landscape opening up and embracing you. That you are allowed in behind what you have just seen.

This is a selection of the stories published in Kofod, Dennis Gade. 2019. *Det levende land*. Copenhagen: Rosinante.

Danish–English translation: Tina Hirschbuehl, 2024.

Bornholm in Pictures II

18 Folkemødet, the biggest political festival in Denmark, is held in Allinge, Bornholm. The three-day festival has been held annually since 2011, and draws large crowds. In 2023, 2,800 events were staged across 200 venues. Photo: Semko Balcerski / Destination Bornholm.

19 Hammershus and to the right, the Obelisk. Photo: Semko Balcerski / Destination Bornholm.

20 Several pilts still exist in Bornholm's landscape and rocks are still being added to some, such as Middle Pilt (*Midterpilt*), which occupies a dominant position in the Paradise Hills some five kilometres east of Varparna.

21 One of the questions in the Danish citizenship test of November 2022: "Who wrote the novels *Pelle the Conqueror* and *Ditte, Child of Man*, at the start of the 1900s?" To pass the test, applicants must answer at least 36 out of the 45 questions correctly, including 4 correct answers out of 5 questions on Danish values. Source: Styrelsen for International Rekruttering og Integration/dr.dk.

22 The author of *Pelle the Conqueror* grew up just outside Nexø
– and adopted the name of the town as his own.

23 Reviving the appeal. Martin Andersen Nexø is now featured in a series of Danish literary walks (danskedigterruter.dk). The literary walks project was launched in 2020, with the aim of strengthening the "conversation between literature, local landscapes, and popular interest". By following the routes, people will "walk, sense, feel, read, and experience, while at the same time soaking up Danish literature, narrative forms, places, and landscape types," according to the University of Southern Denmark, which led the project.

24 The changed face of Vang. Where once hardened quarrymen, stonecutters, masons, and carvers plied their craft, today's hikers get a thrill from peering through the grate that forms the floor of the bridge built in 2002 by artist Peter Bonnén.

25 Til Minde om Vangs Stenhuggere (In memory of the stone-masons of Vang), 1896–1967, a monument created in 1984 by the citizens of Vang. As the information board explains to visitors, the stones displayed ones that broke during work. When this happened, it was usually a financial disaster for the stonemason, as it meant a loss of earnings.

26 The reunification stone in Allinge-Sandvig. One of two stones erected on Bornholm to commemorate the reunification of Southern Jutland with Denmark in 1920. Hundreds of stones were placed throughout Denmark following reunification, to promote a sense of community also in further flung parts of the country. Shaped as a cube, this particular stone was unique in that it was intended to demonstrate the stonemason's ability to work granite.

Part IV – LITERATURE

7 How Pelle Continues to Conquer

One of Denmark's greatest writers spent his formative years on Bornholm. Internationally, he was for a time second only to Denmark's most famous literary export, fairy-tale writer Hans Christian Andersen. His works are required reading in Danish schools, and one thing is clear: knowing the name of the author of "Pelle the Conqueror" would have scored you a point in the Danish citizenship test of November 2022. If that title rings a bell – it was also the name of the multi-award-winning film that won the 1988 Palme d'Or in Cannes, and both an Oscar and a Golden Globe in 1989. But before "Pelle the Conqueror" the film came "Pelle Erobreren" the novel, the story of an immigrant farm labourer's son in rural Denmark in the late 19th century, published in four volumes between 1906 and 1910. And the author is Martin Andersen Nexø (1869–1954), whose childhood home on Bornholm is now a museum along the route of a new literary walk. It seems, then, that his writing still strikes a chord – why? And how did growing up on Bornholm influence his work? These are some of the questions I put to Denmark's foremost expert on the author, Henrik Yde.

Interview with Henrik Yde

The four volumes of Martin Andersen Nexø's novel, *Pelle Erobreren,* as it was called in Danish, were hugely popular when they were published between 1906 and 1910. Within a few years of publication, the novel had an international distribution rivalled only by HC Andersen's fairy tales. Soon after, *Pelle the Conqueror* became the most widespread Danish literary work in the world, not least because it was also published in serial editions in European newspapers of the Labour movement. During and after the First World War, Nexø consolidated his world fame with the novel *Ditte Menneskebarn* – whose title in English is *Ditte, Child of Man* – a five-volume work published between 1917 and 1921, which achieved similar global distribution.

Almost all Nexø's works have been translated into several languages, and several of them are still being reprinted in many countries. His complete works are available in German and Russian. Both *Pelle the Conqueror* and *Ditte, Child of Man* are now available in more than 20 European and Asian languages, and new editions are constantly being published. *Pelle the Conqueror* has recently been translated into Icelandic, and *Ditte, Child of Man* into Vietnamese. His work is most widely read in Germany, both during Nexø's lifetime, and later.

An online search reveals that there's not much information about him in English. In fact, the current Wikipedia entry states that "Pelle the Conqueror" is not a popular novel in the English-speaking world. What are the reasons for this?

In continental northern Europe, the novel appeared as a serial in huge editions in the working-class press, first in several German-speaking countries in 1911–12, then in eight other languages.

The book editions only came later. An English-language translation appeared in 1913–1917, but the novel wasn't featured in the working-class press in Britain, North America, or Australia. Here, only the book editions were published. Following Bille August's acclaimed film, a partial new translation appeared in the US in1991, but only of the first two volumes, after which this project came to a standstill.

What are the ingredients that made his stories so successful?

If you read Martin Andersen Nexø from the beginning – that is, from his first collection of stories, *Skygger (Shadows)*, published in 1898 – you'll find an author with a passion for social issues. An author who is stylistically advanced, and has mastered the tools of Realism, Impressionism, and Symbolism. And an author in deep literary dialogue with 2,000 years of religious, philosophical, and literary traditions, from the Bible to classical European novelists. Nexø had a close relationship with the works of Miguel de Cervantes, Victor Hugo, and Fyodor Dostoyevsky – as well as with the writing of his contemporary, the Danish writer, Henrik Pontoppidan.

In fact, though the two Danish writers never met, Nexø dedicated the entirety of the four-volume *Pelle the Conqueror* "To the Master, Henrik Pontoppidan". Pontoppidan is the author of *Lykke-Per,* and won the Nobel Prize for Literature in 1917 for his descriptions of life in Denmark. Incidentally, *Lykke-Per*, initially translated as "Lucky Per", has been re-translated as "A Fortunate Man" and was made into a film by Bille August in 2018.

At his best, Martin Andersen Nexø produced great art: world literature worth reading even today – and in an unforeseeable future.

There was a time when Nexø's popularity waned in the West…

That's right – after the Russian Revolution, especially from 1937, he became involved in Communist politics, and regarded the Soviet Union as the place of "real socialism". It damaged his credibility and legacy that even during the worst of times under Stalin, he defended the Soviet Union so stubbornly, blindly, and naively. In the last three years of his life, he lived as an honorary citizen in Dresden, East Germany.

He has thus mostly been reduced to being a social realist author. Critics focus on his political positions as an old man, when he no longer wrote fiction worth reading.

As a young man, Nexø was politically active in the left liberal milieu around the daily Danish newspaper, *Politiken*, but he wasn't a member of any party. After the publication of *Pelle Erobreren*, he felt connected to the Labour movement, and joined the Social Democratic Party, which hailed him as the party's poet. In the 1930s, he became a prominent figure in the international anti-fascist movement.

Many critics have been unable to reconcile the social and humanist visions of his fiction writing, on the one hand, with the older Nexø's uncompromising defence of the Soviet Union, on the other.

The fact that a new literary walk is dedicated to him in Denmark would suggest that his works are being rediscovered.

If Nexø's contemporary readers – probably especially those who are too young to have experienced the Cold War – don't seem particularly interested in his relationship with the Soviet Union, it may be due to an intuitive sense that his political views have little to do with his writing.

And they would be right – because Nexø wasn't a communist writer: he was a writer who became communist.

Nexø's writing wasn't formed by the Soviet Union, let alone by the German Democratic Republic. Nexø's world fame as a literary giant was sealed with the spread of *Pelle the Conqueror* in many languages and in many countries before the First World War, long before the Russian Revolution of 1917, and even longer before the founding of the GDR in 1949.

What's *Pelle the Conqueror* about?

Pelle the Conqueror is a four-volume novel published between 1906 and 1910. It depicts Pelle's youth and development at around the turn of the century, between the 1800s and 1900s. Pelle, who is eight years old at the start of the novel, was born in Sweden into a poor farming community. After the death of his mother, Bengta, his father, Lasse, sells their home, and they travel to Bornholm, where Lasse once worked as a young man and earned a good living.

As soon as they arrive, it becomes clear that Bornholm isn't as Lasse remembers. Now quite old and with Pelle too young to work, Lasse gets a poorly paid job as a herdsman at Stone Farm, a large manor house, where he and the boy have to sleep in a small bare room in the stable. This is where Pelle grows up. They are at the bottom of the hierarchy – and Pelle becomes aware of the differences in class. And being Swedish, they are looked down on as immigrants. However, Pelle's childhood is also marked by the strong love and protection that his father tries to give him, and he becomes good at his job as a herdboy, and works hard to gain respect at the village school.

Eventually, Pelle turns his back on working the land and heads to the market town of Rønne, becoming an apprenticed cobbler. Bornholm and Rønne are depicted as a backward, pre-industrial society, and the town's workshops survive only with difficulty. The work is gruelling, and just as on the farm, Pelle is once again acutely aware of the class differences.

The industrialization of shoemaking brings to Rønne not progress, but the death of craftsmanship— and the import of cheap, machine-made shoes. After completing his apprenticeship and starving for a while, Pelle heads for the capital, Copenhagen. He thus completes, on a personal level, the historical migration from country to city in the early phase of industrialization in Denmark. From the beginning of the novel, Pelle's old father, Lasse, has had fairy-tale dreams about Pelle's predestination to happiness.

Source: Adapted from teaching material on *Pelle the Conqueror* for high schools, available at martinander-sennexoe.dk (in Danish).

In a preface to the 1913 English translation of "Pelle the Conqueror", Otto Jespersen, Professor of English at the University of Copenhagen, wrote: "The great charm of the book seems to me to lie in the fact that the writer knows the poor from within; he has not studied them as an outsider may, but has lived with them and felt with them, at once a participant and a keen-eyed spectator... his sympathy is of the widest, and he makes us see tragedies behind the little comedies, and comedies behind the little tragedies, of the seemingly sordid lives of the working people whom he loves." Many years later, Martin Andersen Nexø said that

*he thought the shadows of childhood covered one's whole life.
To what extent did his own childhood influence his writing?*

Martin was born in 1869 into extreme poverty, as the fourth of ten children.

He spent the first three years of his life in a slum in the Christianshavn area of Copenhagen. Today, it's a lively, trendy area – but at the time, it was dirty, dilapidated, overcrowded, and dangerous for people's health. To prevent rats from getting at their food, in the evenings, Martin's mother would hoist it up under the ceiling in a basket.

In 1872, the family moved to the Medical Association's Residences in Østerbro. This was Denmark's first social or non-profit housing development, and it was intended to reduce the contagious overcrowding in the city's poor neighbourhoods, and provide healthy and affordable housing for the disadvantaged. It was built in direct response to the cholera epidemic that had ravaged Danish cities, particularly Copenhagen, where in 1853 it claimed 4,732 lives, or between five and six percent of the city's population, with the highest mortality among the poor. Cholera is a contagious intestinal infection that causes severe diarrhoea which can lead to fatal dehydration, and the infection had good conditions for growth in the city's overpopulated slums. New epidemics broke out in 1854, 1855, and 1857, and something had to be done.

This housing development still exists today. It is now officially known as Brumleby, which was its nickname at the time Martin and his family lived there. Back then, this part of Østerbro was still on the outskirts of Copenhagen, with green fields on one side. For Martin's family, it was like moving from darkness into light.

In 1875, the dwellings housed about 2,000 residents, most of whom had come straight from the slums. To maintain general domestic order and morality, the Medical Association had employed an inspector with the power to dismiss residents for disorder, disrupting the peace, or untrustworthiness. And he did so for up to 50 tenancies a year – about one a week. At the time, tenants had no legal rights against landlords.

But the inhabitants of Brumleby were not just unruly rabble-rousers. We should note that people living there were among the pioneers of the Copenhagen Labour movement, and that the Social Democratic Party Association of Østerbro had its origins here.

So being born into poverty like that set the scene for Martin's novels, and for his later political activity as a committed communist.

Yes. And there's another very important point: the family loved to read. Martin's mother has described how her husband spent all his free time reading whatever he could get his hands on, and that the family owned a number of books. This was unusual for a working-class family in those days. At the time, books were more common in the homes of workers with vocational training, such as typographers, but Martin's father was untrained.

And living in Brumleby, young Martin had access to a library, whose records show that he borrowed, among other publications, *The Last of the Mohicans* by James Fenimore Cooper; two comedies by Ludvig Holberg; and ecclesiastical writings by NFS Grundtvig.

I am assuming, then, that it was important for Martin's parents to send him to school?

After first attending the nearby day-care – which was free for the poorest families, thanks to subsidies and benefactors – in 1876, Martin was enrolled in Sankt Hansgades Skole, a *friskole*, or non-fee-paying school. The purpose of this type of school was to educate children, especially those from poor homes, in discipline and obedience, which, it was believed, were lacking at home. Teacher authority was maintained not least by means of flogging. The school's pedagogy was still predominantly influenced by the ideas of the conservative German pedagogue and neo-Kantian philosopher JF Herbart. He believed that schools should mould children into rational individuals, and that if the children's will did not bend willingly, corporal punishment should be used.

Needless to say, this time was not a happy one for Nexø, who wrote of the beatings, torment, and harassment. He has a soft spot for his singing teacher, AH Viggo Sonne, in whose classes, as Martin notes in his memoirs, "We really made an effort. But if we sang the wrong way, even he knew no other response than to hit us on the head with the end of the violin bow."

But the crowded conditions in class and at home were unhealthy, and a very large proportion of Copenhagen schoolboys suffered from scrofula – a tuberculosis of the lymphatic glands.

And then, in 1877, unemployment soared, leading to hunger and destitution among Copenhagen's proletariat. The policy at the time was to send people back to where they had come from. As Martin's father hailed from Bornholm, this is where they went.

Moving to Bornholm – which, at the time, involved a 20-hour boat ride from Copenhagen – must have been a huge event, perhaps even disruption, in the family's life.

For his family, the journey to Bornholm represented the transition from a prospectless existence in the shadow of unemployment, to new hope. But it was also a brutal transition, from life in the large, modern, industrial city of Copenhagen, to the small town of Nexø, in faraway Bornholm.

In one volume of his memoirs, *Under an Open Sky*, Nexø describes the agony of seasickness during 20 hours at high sea: this dramatic interpretation was a fitting introduction to the family's new life. "The tension of our departure hammered at my throat and head and rushed around in my ears," Nexø remembers. A look in the archives shows, however, that the "small boneshaker" of a boat that Martin described was in reality a state-of-the-art steamship, the *SS Erna*, and that on the day they travelled, the sea was calm.

"Pelle was perfectly well aware that even the poorest boys there always wore their best clothes, and ate bread-and-dripping with sugar on it as often as they liked. There, money lay like dirt by the roadside, and the Bornholmers did not even take the trouble to stoop and pick it up; but Pelle meant to pick it up..."

Pelle the Conqueror, shortly after Lasse and Pelle arrive on Bornholm in the 1870s. Did Martin Andersen Nexø have similar expectations when he arrived on the island as a young boy?

So Martin, now eight, arrives on Bornholm, to a new life. The start of "Pelle the Conqueror" springs to mind, when eight-year-old Pelle arrives with his father from Sweden, and Nexø describes the islanders thus: "It was only their usual secretiveness, their inveterate distrust of everyone who did not speak their dialect and look exactly like them." Is this what Martin experienced? How was the Andersen family received on Bornholm?

In his memoirs, Martin speaks of the distrust the Andersen family encountered, as foreigners on the island. Having a father who was from the island helped – but he said it still took years to become accepted in the island community.

Martin also mentions that his family wasn't devout enough for the Bornholmers' liking. So as not to stick out, his mother sent the children to Sunday School. But they were signed up to the Lutheran Mission rather than to the parish church; whether this was by accident or on purpose isn't clear.

How did that affect Martin?

Certainly, his works were influenced by the religious pressure he experienced in the Lutheran Mission's Pietistic Sunday School in Nexø. He wrote that as a small boy, this strict, Pietistic Christianity kept him awake many a night: the fear of the highly uncertain hereafter, of God's judgement, of eternal damnation. He was therefore delighted to discover the joyful Christianity of Grundtvigianism, enabling him to rejoice in life, as well as in the perception of the hereafter.

Martin adopted the name of the town the family lived in – Nexø – as his own, and was from then on known as Martin Andersen Nexø. How did this come about?

In 1894, he started signing his letters Martin Andersen-Nexø – initially, with a hyphen; from 1898, without. Nexø himself said a bookseller had told him that Andersen was a bad name for a writer – unless of course you were the famous Hans Christian Andersen. Because books by any other author whose surname started with "A" would be placed on the highest shelf in bookshops – and not at eye-level, like authors with names starting in the middle of the alphabet.

But that might not be the whole explanation. It was quite common for men with names ending in "-sen" (-son, in English) to differentiate themselves by adding another name, such as the place they were from. A few of his contemporaries did the same, including fellow writer Jeppe Jensen, from Aakjær, who went by the name Jeppe Aakjær.

So the name change was actually done more for practical considerations than because this was a particularly happy time in his life?

Well, it probably was the best time in the family's life. Initially, Martin's father, Hans Jørgen Andersen, got a good job laying cobblestones. They no longer had to live from hand to mouth, as had been the case in Copenhagen – and they were able to save some money. On Nexø town square you can still see the stone on which Hans Jørgen proudly signed his work, "HA".

Several years after moving to Bornholm, the Andersen family managed to climb the social hierarchy. Martin's father had saved up enough to buy a plot of land and build a house for the family, and, for a while, they became a part of the town's petite bourgeoisie. But things started to go seriously downhill at the start of the new century, when the company Hans Jørgen had been working for went bankrupt, leaving Hans Jørgen not only unemployed, but also slipping into alcoholism.

By 1902, the family had to give up the house they had built in Ferskesøstræde. Martin's parents moved back to Copenhagen and separated. The house was listed in 1983. Since 1990, it has been home to the Martin Andersen Nexø museum.

By the time his parents left the island, Martin had already long gone. He lived on Bornholm for 14 years, from 1877 to 1891. What was life like on the island for Martin?

Corporal punishment was still rife at Martin's new school, the public school in Nexø. Academically, he was a good student, ranking third out of 22 pupils in the class. He was so good that he was able to skip a year, finishing school in six years, rather than the usual seven.

He then worked as a herdboy, an experience that later provided the background for the detailed descriptions of Pelle's herding job in the first volume (*Boyhood*) of *Pelle the Conqueror*. These five months in 1883, possibly more, were an important time in his life. Not only was it his first experience of nature up close – plants and animals, rocks and soil, changing weather and seasons – it was also good for his health. Like so many other boys from the Copenhagen slums, he had suffered from lymph gland tuberculosis. Now he was gaining strength. And there were three more important points: he had plenty to eat at this particular farm; he learned how to control the cattle – even the farm's mighty bull had to learn to obey a skinny 14-year-old boy; and finally – to judge by his memoirs – he seems to have been a valued member of the farm, and the praise he got there gave him a whole new level of self-confidence.

The year after, in 1884, Martin was apprenticed to a shoemaker. But this profession was to hold no future for him. In the late 1880s, Danish shoemakers who still plied their craft by hand faced disastrous competition from German and Danish shoe manufacturers. Danish shoe factories still used skilled shoemakers to operate the only partially mechanized tools, but it was only a matter of time before steam power was introduced in the 1890s, replacing the skilled shoemakers with unskilled labour.

Nexø's great leap from manual to intellectual labour was made possible by the support of local patrons, who enabled his return to education at Østermarie Højskole on Bornholm in 1890–1891, and then in Jutland, at Askov extended Højskole, in 1891–1893. In Askov, he found a home with Mathilde Molbech, widow of the late Romantic poet, Christian Knud Frederik Molbech. After finishing his studies at the folk high school, he found work as a teacher at various schools in the Grundtvig tradition. He later acknowledged his gratitude to Grundtvigianism, and his admiration for NFS Grundtvig through changing ideological circumstances, describing Grundtvig as "the most far-sighted spirit Denmark has produced." As mentioned, Grundtvigianism prescribed a joyful Christianity, and was in great contrast to the strict Pietism of the Lutheran Mission of his childhood.

Later, the character he created, Pelle, was to undertake exactly the same jobs, which Martin, with his experience, was equipped to describe in meticulous and accurate detail.

For a while in his early 20s, Martin worked as a teacher in Odense. Unexpectedly, this was where he got his writing debut, when in 1893, the local newspaper, Fyns Tidende, published his article on a tradition from faraway Bornholm.

Yes, Martin knew the editor, but it was still surprising that a completely unknown young writer was allowed to fill the front page of a medium-sized newspaper from the island of Funen with a description of folk life from distant Bornholm.

When the article – "Midsummer's Eve (St Hansaften) on Bornholm. A Snapshot" – was published, 24-year-old Martin the teacher couldn't have known that he had laid the cornerstone for his literary career. But writing was a natural side job in teaching circles. And now, one of these writing teachers, Martin Andersen, had been published – with a description of a folkloric tradition.

But the article showed that in his debut, Martin Andersen had already brought up two themes that were to reappear throughout his literary career over the next 60 years: the common people's dreams of happiness, and women as upholders of life.

In fact, this debut article also finds its way into the first volume of the work that made him internationally famous – *Pelle Erobreren*. Similarly, a number of the other short articles that Nexø published during 1893–1904 are also incorporated into the book.

Let's talk about "Pelle the Conqueror". The novel traces Pelle's transformation from farm labourer's son to union leader. What are the main themes Nexø wishes to portray across the four volumes?

Through four volumes, we follow the immigrant boy Pelle on the classic journey from country to city, in search of happiness.

> "He had promised himself so much from the island, and it was nothing but worry and toil and trouble – nothing else at all."

> Pelle's father, Lasse, reflects on his situation on Bornholm. He is illiterate and depends on his son's tormentor to read the names of the cows in his care. At this point, he feels sad at being too old to defend Pelle with his fists, despite having promised to do so.

In the common perception of *Pelle the Conqueror*, the novel has most often been positioned as a realistic work whose main theme is contemporary social reality. However, this easily overlooks the fact that the novel – like so many other novels – both directly and indirectly relates to and discusses literary, philosophical, and religious traditions and predecessors.

Nexø succeeded here in a large format – through a synthesis of Grundtvigian, anarchist, and socialist visions – in creating coherence and interaction between two aspects of existence: the spiritual-heroic, conquering, "male" aspect – and a sustaining, caring, corporeal-material, "female" aspect. In the literature he produced as a young man, the masculine ideal seems to fall short: the "ideal family" in his novels and stories is upheld only by strong, natural women, while the men mostly seem decrepit, drunk, degenerate, or decadent.

Nexø was also influenced by Victor Hugo's classic, *Les Misérables*, in particular in the third and fourth volumes of *Pelle the Conqueror* (*The Great Struggle*), for which Nexø conducted a systematic study of the history and spirit of the working class and the Labour movement.

There is no doubt that the novel is also heavily influenced by Martin's own experience. Pelle arrives on Bornholm at the age of eight, he works as a herdboy, and eventually as a shoemaker, before leaving the island for Copenhagen. And Pelle is born on the same day, in the same year, as Martin.

Between 1932 and 39, in his 60s, Nexø published his memoirs, in which he attempts to weigh up what he received from his mother and father, respectively, during his childhood. Ultimately, his poetic responsibility and commitment to humanity seem to stem from gratitude for what he received early on, especially from women.

How was "Pelle the Conqueror" received when it was published?

In Denmark, a four-volume *"People's Edition"* was issued, with a print run of 2,500 copies. This was big for an author whose books had previously been published in editions of between 1,250 and 1,500 copies. But it was to be bigger than anyone could have imagined, and in ways no one had known before.

After finishing *Pelle the Conqueror*, Nexø and his family spent four months in Germany. In Berlin, he contacted *Vorwärts*, a newspaper described as the "central organ of Social Democracy in Germany". The German Social Democratic Party was the leading and largest party in the Second International, the federation of the world's Social Democratic parties between 1889 and 1914. The literary editor of *Vorwärts*, Karsten Heinrich Döscher, agreed to publish all four volumes in serial editions as of January 1911 in the newspaper, which had a circulation of 150,000 at the time. And a further 60 German – Social Democratic – newspapers followed suit. The total circulation of the newspapers that carried *Pelle der Eroberer*, as the story was called in German, is unknown, but certainly reached a readership of millions. In Austria-Hungary, the story was carried by the *Wiener Arbeiterzeitung* and *Volksrecht* of Karlsbad/Karlovy Vary, and in Switzerland, it was featured in *Basler Vorwärts* and *Volksrecht* of Zurich.

The newspaper serialization was followed in 1912 by a book edition, published by Insel-Verlag in Leipzig, and translated by Mathilde Mann, a prolific and well-known translator who had married into the literary Mann family. Despite both the publishing house and translator being among Germany's best, the initial print run was a modest 3,000 copies. Several editions followed during the Weimar Republic of 1919–1933, however, totalling 48,000 copies. In the Nazi era, all remaining editions of Nexø's books were destroyed.

Pelle the publishing phenomenon

Pelle conquers the world in a few fast years. Before and during the First World War, *Pelle the Conqueror* was available in eight languages, besides Danish: German, Norwegian (serial edition from 1912, book edition 1939), French (serial edition of the third volume 1912, abridged book edition 1947), Russian (1912 fragments of the third volume in the journal, Russkoye Bogatsvo, abridged book edition of the same 1924), Swedish (serial from 1913, book edition 1921–1922), Dutch (serial in the Netherlands from 1913, book edition 1926), Flemish (serial in Belgium 1913–1914), and English/American (book edition 1913–1917).

If *Pelle the Conqueror* is seen as a working-class novel, in the sense of a novel for working-class people, its circulation in just a few years as a serial in the European working-class press shows that it very quickly reached this target group. Only later – in some languages, several decades later – did book publications follow. As mentioned above, during Nexø's lifetime, Hans Christian Andersen's fairy tales were the most widely read Danish literary works in the world – and it is often said that *Pelle the Conqueror* was second, albeit only in its serialized editions in the working-class press in the early 20th century, and not in book form.

Pelle the Conqueror is now available in over twenty languages. A 1998 project to translate the novel into Vietnamese was put on hold for financial reasons. The work has its widest circulation in German, and its lowest in Europe in the Romance languages. A Spanish translation was also underway, but halted after the first two volumes were published in 2016–2017.

Source: Yde, H. (2019) *NEXØ: Martin Andersen Nexøs liv og værk*. Lindhardt og Ringhof.

There is no doubt that the prize-winning film version of "Pelle the Conqueror" – which won the Palme d'Or and an Oscar, among many other awards – put this novel and its writer on the map, especially for an English-speaking audience. The actor who played Pelle in the Oscar-winning film, Pelle Hvenegaard, was actually named after the character – despite being born in 1975! Was this a common phenomenon?

It absolutely was. The exact number is not known, but since the novel was published, thousands of Pelles have been born, not only in Denmark, but in other countries as well. In Germany, literary historian Walter A Berendsohn wrote that German workers named their sons Pelle in around 1911–1912, and when a worker was considered by his comrades to be politically alert, action-oriented, and intelligent, he was given the nickname "Pelle".

The same thing happened later with the name of Ditte, the young female protagonist in the five-volume *Ditte, Child of Man*. Pelle and Ditte are striking examples of how certain first names have migrated in large numbers from the world of fiction to the world of reality, because novel readers have identified so strongly with these fictional characters.

"Pelle the Conqueror" is a novel about the Labour movement of the early 20th century. Is the novel still interesting for contemporary readers?

We may ask if it's the sentimental need for stories of innocence – and with happy endings – that still give the work its popularity. In the preface, Nexø hinted that the aim of this novel was to go beyond the history and politics of the time: he declared that this was to be "a book about the proletarian – that is, about man himself".

In Dresden, where Nexø spent the final years of his life, a high school is named after him – now the Martin-Andersen-Nexö Gymnasium Dresden, abbreviated to MANOS after its initial acronym, when it was still an *Oberschule*. An attempt to change the name after the reunification of Germany failed.

At the naming ceremony in 2001, I was invited to give a speech about Nexø. It concluded that, for all Nexø's political aberrations and personal foibles, his writing's exploration of the interplay between male and female, between spirit and matter, between the infinitely small and the infinitely large, and between humanity's near and distant commitments, had produced great poetry that will endure – and besides, that the vision and ethical message underlying the author's major works, about human communities and society as a home governed by love, rather than greed, a society that uses all its members' capacities and, as a matter of course, also takes care of its guardians, is true and important, indeed urgent, then as now.

Henrik Yde is the author of *NEXØ: Martin Andersen Nexøs liv og værk* (NEXØ: The Life and Letters of Martin Andersen Nexø), published in 2019 by Lindhardt og Ringhof.
Interview by Tina Hirschbuehl.

Editor's aside: Martin Andersen Nexø, son of a quarry worker, used to visit the stonemasons in Vang (see the next chapter, by Henning Ipsen). On a recent exploration of Vang with our daughters, my husband, who is Swiss, stopped off for coffee in the small harbour. In friendly conversation with the café owner, he explained that his mother-in-law was from the nearby town of Hasle. Because surely mentioning to a Bornholmer that you, a foreigner, are also in some way connected to Bornholm is bound to be in your favour? Whereupon the café owner in Vang gave a hearty laugh, and said: "We have a saying here in Vang: 'There are three things you shouldn't do: drink, get into debt, and speak to people from Hasle.'"

As we learned, Martin Andersen Nexø wrote about the islanders' suspicion of foreigners. But in 1935, he also wrote the words:

> *Alt i alt er det en god lille Ø. Og det bedste ved den er dens Mennesker.*[5]
> *(All in all, it's a good little island. And the best thing about it is its people.)*

---

5 This quote appears in the 1942 edition of *Jul paa Bornholm* (p. 33), in an article by Christian Stub-Jørgensen. According to the article, which is available via *Bornholms Historiske Samfund* (https://bornholmske-samlinger.dk/), Martin Andersen Nexø wrote the section on Bornholm in HV Clausen's *Danmark* (1935), ending with these words.

8 The Stonemason

Getting to the bottom of who Bornholmers really are isn't just a recent question. Hasle-born writer Henning Ipsen (1930–1984) sought to pen his thoughts on the island he so loved in "Bornholm og Bornholmere" (Bornholm and Bornholmers), a 1967 collection of black-and-white photographs for which Ipsen wrote the words. One of the chapters – "The Stonemason" – describes the harsh conditions under which the quarry workers of the seaside hamlet of Vang worked the unrelenting stone with their hammers, before machines took over the toughest parts of their job.

By Henning Ipsen

At the beginning of the century, Germans owned large parts of north Bornholm. They ran quarries and hotels, and planned a New Berlin near Sandvig, but the War got in the way. There was much quarrying at that time – perhaps too much. These days you have to wonder how long it could have gone on before Hammerknuden, to not just Norwegian but also Danish eyes, became a *hole*.

Some 1,000 men worked in the Hammer quarry alone. Foreign workers came from Sweden, Germany, and Italy (names such as Brantigrani and Rosa were common). The quarries worked on multi-year projects, such as the cladding of Christiansborg Palace[6] and Copenhagen City Hall.

Many boys became apprenticed to stonemasons, and this was a high-performance trade. The manager of Vang Quarry, Anker Hansen, a giant of a man, speaks

---

6 Originally a royal castle, Christiansborg Palace houses *Folketinget*, the Danish Parliament (also known as *Borgen*), so having supplied the building with granite was justifiably a source of pride for Bornholmers.

with the joy of an old craftsman from the years when young carvers competed for the heavy stones – the work was a challenge. When Hansen lays a great big paw of a hand on the rock, his voice softens. Granite is a material with many possibilities; assessing the qualities of a piece requires know-how.

After the flourishing years, the trade stagnated. Today, a headstone can be cut on all four sides with a machine, and then the front can be polished by machine – only the letters remain to be hewn. But there are still craftsmen. In his free time, Hansen works on copies of classical sculptures. Hermes was taking shape during our visit.

After the First World War, production in Vang switched to kerbstones, and that's not much fun for a craftsman.

Vang lies by the sea, below the Ringe Hills. The granite is quarried in the hills above town, in a kettle hole baked by Casablanca sun in the summer. Then, the rocks are yellow, and burning hot. The stone is blasted loose, and transported down to the sea, where it is worked close to the small harbour.

These clear, sunny summer days of clean air and big sky are awash with private home flags, ice-cream booth pennants, and boarding houses offering outdoor service. Amid the multitude of Danish flags, as if to prove a point, the local schooner is named *National*! The crane is hand-operated by a man presumably well beyond blisters.

The wooden grinding hall rumbles throughout the day with the noise of the pneumatic drills and grinding machines. The dust is swallowed by huge built-in vacuum cleaners. The rest of us can escape. The workers cannot. This is their life. That's why one understands the ironic – or tormented – soul who chalked on the wooden walls: "Hell's forecourt". Much is done to ensure people's safety, but the noise is diabolical.

Outside – in wonderful fresh air, in the summer – stonemasons split large blocks for kerbstones. The coarsest work is done by pneumatic drill, then later with wedges and a hammer, before the stones are finally hewn into shape. A young mason in a striped T-shirt, with steel-framed glasses to protect his eyes, jumps acrobatically to catch the small chisel; it hops up in the air every time he drives it down into the drilled holes. Even this hard work can become a bit of a game. When he has hammered long enough, the block splits vertically.

Behind one of the screens facing the sea that summer, and many previously, stands Wollmar, full name Erik Wollmar Tolvte Carlsson, twelfth child of one of the Swedish immigrant workers. Wollmar's father received a plot of land up in the hills from a quarry owner responsible for supplying workers for the place. The union was founded by Carlsson the elder, who was its chairman for 25 years. Wollmar was then chair for 19 years, and his brother Walter for eight years. The Chiseller and Cobblestonemason's Association in Vang has been a family business.

All twelve children in the Carlsson family, including the girls, had to help in the quarry, carry tools down over the rocks from the higher Ringe area to the smithy, drive its bellows, and drag smaller stones back and forth. Wollmar Carlsson started at the age of 11. He can recount the story of his brother, whose hands were so ravaged by the coarse granite that the town's children – unfamiliar with the similar hands of trapeze artists – showed off his hands, to shudders all round. No one was mollycoddled much; when Wollmar ended up with a long gash across his wrist (the scar is still visible) from a sharp edge, old Carlsson shook the quarry dust from the rag in his pocket, and bound it round the wound. And yet Wollmar Carlsson speaks without bitterness about a father who was strong and hardy, but who could also sweep all work aside and tell stories (as he also did for Andersen Nexø), or take out his accordion for a song and dance.

All work was done by hand in those years. It has become easier over time, but still involves heavy "lifts", when a man has to heave a kerbstone's many kilos up onto the block for dressing. During the war, many of the workers had to start their own private production operations with limited engine power. Wollmar worked stone above Vang using an abandoned airplane engine to power his operation – when fuel was available.

The work is piecework. Every week, a man's output is measured in metres. Of course, most is achieved when the quality of stone is good, and on the whole, Wollmar Carlsson was able to take home a weekly wage of about 400 kroners to his Jutland-born wife, Sofie. Both are members of the little Baptist congregation in Vang.

One beautiful summer's eve, as we drove from Vang, the air was clean, the sky blue. A breeze rippled through the pink wheat. Sweden's houses shone from across the sea, and one could see Skåne's eastern corner with the naked eye. Down in Vang, the pneumatic hammer was silent. At moments like this, it's so easy to forget that granite can be hard and stubborn.

PS: But we remembered again, when we returned in March. The air was wet. The wind was strong. Inside the grinding hall hung a clammy depression. The worker's eyes had dimmed. "Cold?" they said, breaking into a pale smile. "It's been many years since we've been able to stand like this on 10th March." Because of the weather, they'd been unemployed since "Little Christmas Eve"[7] until 1st March. Also: the Portuguese nicked the work for the Little Belt Bridge from us. We thought there would be a lot."

---

7 *Lillejuleaften*, or "Little Christmas Eve", is 23rd December.

In a small town, people feel the loss of a large contract. Portugal can play a role in Vang.

And Wollmar Carlsson, born in 1907, has hung up his boots. His tough constitution couldn't endure this work after all. After a long period of ill-health, he had to seek a disability pension – hard for an active man and great storyteller who can tell of Andersen Nexø's stay in Vang. It has become easier to work with stone since Wollmar Carlsson started out as a boy, but it's still a tough job. It's no longer a Nexø story – as Carlsson's family background was – but granite is still stubborn and heavy enough to break work-hardened menfolk.

Original Danish text: Ipsen, Henning. 1967. Stenhuggeren. *In:* Ipsen, H and Jonsson, S. 1967. *Bornholm og Bornholmere*. Fremad, pp. 47–62.

Danish–English translation: Tina Hirschbuehl, 2024.

Editor's aside: Bornholm is the location of two *genforeningssten* – commemorative reunification stones – that were erected throughout Denmark to mark the reunification of Sønderjylland – some 470 km from Bornholm! – with Denmark, on 9 June 1920. Southern Jutland (Sønderjylland) had been German (and called North Schleswig) since Denmark's defeat in the Second Schleswig War of 1864. On Bornholm, one stone is in Christianshøj, near Aakirkeby (Segenvej 48), and the other is in Allinge-Sandvig (Strandvejen 27). The latter is unique, in that it differs in form and shape from most of the other stones erected: its cubic shape and individually carved sides were intended to showcase the stonemason's ability to work granite.

9 Two Short Stories

Both of the following – "Da jeg begyndte at vinterbade" (When I Started Winter Bathing) and "Den sidste fisker" (The Last Fisherman) – were first published in "Øer" (Islands), a collection of short stories by Nexø-raised Bornholmer Rakel Haslund-Gjerrild, whose writing has been published to great acclaim in Denmark. This is the first time they have been published in an English translation.

By Rakel Haslund-Gjerrild

When I Started Winter Bathing

When Marie died, my life changed in two significant ways: I developed tinnitus, and then I started winter bathing. There's not much to say about tinnitus. Many people suffer from it, and they understand without words, and those that don't will never understand, until they get it themselves. Mine sounds like lorries revving up. There are days when the noise is minimal. Smooth wheels on soft, German motorways. But when it's bad, it's like standing on a road with loose chippings, where enormous lorries of Eastern European origin hurtle back and forth. The only time I really escape from the engine noise in my ear is when I dive into the sea, and that's the main reason I started winter bathing.

The thing is, I only go bathing at night. I've always got up early, and now that I'm old, it's so early that you might as well say I get up at night. I don't eat – just throw on some clothes, and then pull out the bicycle. It's my wife's old one. My own broke a year ago, and besides, hers has a good basket, in which I place the towel and the keys. The beach is five kilometres outside of town, and it's quite dark, as the main road is the only place the municipality found money to keep the streetlights on after midnight. But I'd be able to cycle to the beach blindfold. We've gone there our whole lives: when we were young, then with the kids, later on, the two of us oldies, and now me alone.

My children say I look better, rosy cheeks, clearer eyes, and then they say that there are probably many years left in me. They wonder, I know, whether they've perhaps misunderstood my and Marie's relationship, which of course makes me a bit sad. It's just that I don't think I can tell my children about the nightly outings, as this would make them worry, and also, it feels like this winter bathing thing is something deeply private. I don't think I would be able to explain it to them. I'm a bashful man, and even though I haven't yet met another night bather on my outings, I always used to wear bathing trunks. Every time. Even though it's actually a bit of a bother to get the sticky, ice-cold, rubber garment off, especially when you have to be careful not to take too long about it. But last season, during one of the very cold February nights, my bathing trunks froze to the bridge. I had brought ski pants and Irish coffee, as it was my wife's birthday, and also clear and frosty. After I had been in the sea, I sat down in my ski pants on the bench at the end of the jetty, and drank a toast to Marie. When I was about to start packing up, I tore at the bathing trunks without thinking, and there I was, a mere shred to my name. Now, I creep in completely naked. For a moment, I float, like a white buoy between a black sea and a black sky. I don't always submerge my whole head. I save it for the especially tough days, when my brain is so busy that I only see a motion blur when I try to think. As I lower my head under the water, it's as if the sea is hammering an awl through my forehead, and everything in me is screaming, but then it becomes totally still.

Later, the lorries start up again. They are still hesitant, and sound a bit rusty after the ice water – I usually manage to get out to the main road, and a fair way down it, before they really get going. Occasionally, like now, when spring is approaching, and especially if I am late getting out the door, so that on the way home, I glimpse the early light of dawn on the horizon, I might take the cycle path along the coast. I cycle on the embankment, above the black heather and the lighter-coloured stones that the waves wash over when it's windy. It's really a narrow, uneven path, so shrunk by the dark that there's hardly space even for the narrow wheels of my wife's bicycle, let alone large vehicles. So I cycle extra slowly, and enjoy the peace and the disappearing darkness all the way home.

The Last Fisherman

Dad stops the engine. There's no wind. Only tiny waves lap alongside the fishing boat, *Betty*. Nick lies on the bench behind Dad, with his head on Dad's fleece. They told Mum they'd be back before lunch, but that was a long time ago, and Nick got so hungry that he ate the last of the rolls, and Dad's still sailing. Dad suggests that Nick should take a nap, but Nick can't sleep. He just lies there, looking out into the cabin, picking splinters off the folding table. Dad turns to the islands behind them, and the houses in his eyes shine like a sunflower field in the afternoon light.

"If anyone comes, we'll sail back to Nexø," Dad says, jumping down from the swivel chair. He stops in the doorway on his way out onto the deck, and looks at Nick. "You take the wheel, Nick."

When they lived on Christiansø, Nick, Stine, and Mum often went out with Dad to haul the nets. Sometimes, especially if Mum was at work over on Bornholm, Dad would let Nick skip school and go with him. In return, Nick would have to read aloud to Dad, while Dad sailed out to the nets. But then they had to move to Nexø. Dad said it was impossible to fish at Christiansø, the way it was now. The best thing about moving is the role-playing games. There are three kids in Nick's new class who also play. The worst thing is that Dad no longer takes Nick out, even though Dad now also goes fishing on weekends. Today is the first time since they moved that Nick has come out, too. He woke up right away, when Dad whispered to him at four-thirty in the morning that they were leaving. Dad had found Nick's down jacket and winter boots, even though Mum had put them up in the attic.

"It's cold at sea," says Dad, and packs the flask, while Nick puts on his slightly too small boots. Dad doesn't have to mark the map or anything, to know where he's put out the nets. They cast off in the pitch dark, and as dawn breaks, the boat is ready at the small red buoys. They eat breakfast inside the cabin, buns with cheese and butter and coffee in metal mugs, before pulling up the nets. Dad gets up, and brushes the crumbs from the table into his hand, and throws them out of the window. Nick puts his down jacket back on, and a life vest on top. Dad zips up his fleece, but doesn't put on a jacket.

When they're at sea, Nick's job is to help Dad pick cod from the net, and make sure the emptied net is spread out, and packed into the bags. The sound of cod is smooth and squirming; suddenly they're everywhere. You have to be quick. The net-hauler pulls up the wet net of gasping cod whose gills have got stuck in the netting. Dad disentangles the cod quickly, and tosses them into the hatch on the deck. Sometimes, the wet, slimy bodies slip through his hands, and then it's Nick's job to catch the struggling cod. But today, Dad stands strangely still, hands down at his sides, just letting the nets and cod glide past him onto the deck, in a tangled pile. The nets are covered in small scales, and fins and tails drop from the mesh, and onto the deck next to Nick's boots. The deck planks shine. They are greased with a mixture of white meat and lumps of blueish-purple blood, and bits of soft, pink liver. There are small pearly-grey scales everywhere, reflecting the sun where its rays hit the deck. A few individual cod thump their tails, and writhe around in the mire. Dad picks one up. It has scratches down its side, but it isn't dead yet. Dad throws it over the railing. When Dad has finished throwing out cod heads and cod tails, they have a small box with six good cod. They like the stomachs best, right where the liver and other innards are. It's so easy for them to rip open the nets, and then munch away. Dad squats, and examines the tears in the net. There's steam coming from his face and from the orange overalls, in the blue morning light. It's just like a buffet for them, Dad said, that time they moved from Christiansø.

Now they're just sailing. Dad sits at the wheel, and says nothing. Nick goes around as he pleases. He pours ice onto their cod in the fish box; Dad had forgotten. He finds a fish head on the deck. With his fingers, he can feel how the seal's teeth have torn the fish apart. When he and Dad clean cod, they cut off the head with a sharp knife, which Dad keeps in his belt. It slides through the fish like a samurai sword, until you get to the neck vertebrae. You need to put your strength into it, but afterwards, the cut looks all clean and fine. In the head that the seals tore off, the spine wasn't bitten through properly at the neck, but sticks out of the head, stripped of skin and flesh. He looks the cod in the eye, one at a time. They are big and amber-coloured, and the pupil is perhaps a little uneven, but he can't see any fear of being ripped apart by a big, fat seal. It looks just as plain dead as the good cod in the fish box.

As it warms up during the course of the morning, Nick puts his down jacket into the cabin with Dad. There are three buns left over from this morning, and Dad has a cupboard containing Nescafé and jam. Nick eats one bun himself, and spreads jam on the others for Dad, who just looks down at the four halves with strawberry. "No thanks," says Dad, then changes course towards starboard, and away from Nexø again. Nick thinks they're sailing in big circles. He's sitting on the bench behind Dad, who is leaning in over the wheel, like a large, heavy shadow.

"Take a nap, Nick. We were up early," says Dad, smiling a little wryly at Nick on the bench. Nick lays his head on his dad's fleece, but he's not tired. It's like the time they moved from Christiansø, when Dad said it would be good for them all to live on Bornholm, but his face was all dark, and then he left, and only came back the next morning.

You take the wheel, said Dad, as he walked out onto the deck, and now Nick sits on the swivel chair with the wheel in his hands. Like sitting on a throne and keeping an eye on everything, that's what Dad had said, is what it's like sitting in the red swivel chair, with the wheel before you, and the sea on all sides. They are just north of Frederiksø. Lilletårn's pointy black roof sticks up like a pencil from the rocky island behind them. They've not seen other boats out today. Dad was the last of the fishermen to move from the islands. Nick's friend Andreas got a rowing boat for his birthday. They used it to sail out to Tyveskær and Præsteskær to build a campfire, find bird's eggs, or watch the seals. Now *Betty* lies between the island of Græsholm and Vesterskær, where all the seals are. The boat rocks a little, but doesn't drift, as there is no wind, and the current isn't particularly strong today. Dad stands completely still at the bow, watching the seals. They're big. Post-Lars, who has a hunting licence, shot a seal every now and then, and then the boys were allowed to help skin it. It's not the same as cleaning cod. The biggest one Post-Lars took home weighed more than 300 kilos. Nick and Andreas had a plan: in secret, they saved a sealskin from being thrown out, cut it into small pieces and fed Post-Lars's big German Shepherd with it, so it could go wild with the taste of seal, and hunt seals itself. Suddenly, Dad has a rifle in his hands. Nick's skin tingles all over, as if there are ants crawling around his fingers and his back. Nick didn't know his dad had a rifle. His stomach churns. He looks back towards Frederiksø, but there are no boats yet leaving the harbour. A gunshot rings out. A flock of seagulls flaps up, and flies screaming across the sea. Now Nick can see that his dad is still at the bow, and that the rifle is pointing towards the seals at Græsholm. Now it's completely still, and the seals are lying as if they're all dead, or as if they haven't at all noticed anything, and are just relaxing in the warmth of the sun. Then, one of the biggest lifts its fat neck with the small round head, and snorts steam and spit towards *Betty*. It opens its mouth, and the other seals on the island lift their heads. Suddenly, with a roar, the whole island is in motion. The sun goes into Nick's eyes, so that Dad looks like a thin line, like the sight of a rifle, at the end of the bow. The rifle sounds again, and the big, roaring leader-seal's neck snaps the wrong way back, making blood spurt out the back of its head. The stone dust lifts as the body hits the rock with a thump. It hangs motionless in the air for a moment, but then all the island's seals writhe around at once and spit and steam and kick up so much dust that the air looks muddy above them. Waves form as the seals in the front rows plop into the sea, and on top of them come the next ones, if Dad doesn't manage to shoot them. The wheel shakes in Nick's hands. There are seven to eight seals left on the stony beach. One was shot where the flipper joins the shoulder. It can't get up, and has to writhe around in semi-circles. It's bleeding a lot, and smears out blood like black snow-angel wings on the light grey stone. Now Dad shoots the ones that are swimming. They're harder to hit in the sea. Many of the bullets disappear soundlessly into the sea, but once in a while, a smooth, silver-skinned back brakes hard, as if it had swum into an underwater reef. Then, it lies still on the surface of the sea, until it slowly sinks. Dad lowers the rifle. Nick takes a hurried look back. Lilletårn still stands completely still, the black pointy roof and the thick, round body looking like a big cartridge. There are still no other boats around. Nick can feel his cold trousers, wet with pee, sticking to his legs, but he doesn't dare let go of the wheel, as Dad is still standing out there, waiting. They both see it at the same time. The head that suddenly sticks up out of the water not that far from *Betty*. It turns its round head to the left and to the right to look about. Dad lifts the rifle. Nick can see its face, the beard and the long eyelashes, which are dripping sun-glistened drops of sea water back into the sea. Dad hits it as it closes its eyes, or else it closes its eyes because Dad hits it. It is flung back; its light-coloured belly turns upwards, and then it lies there, floating.

Original Danish texts in Haslund-Gjerrild, Rakel. 2016. *Øer*. Askeby: Kronstork.

Danish–English translation: Tina Hirschbuehl, 2024.

Epilogue

By Tina Hirschbuehl

In Chapter 1, Jens mentions mass immigration of Bornholmers to the US. That made me curious as to whether there were places called "Bornholm" there, or anywhere else in the world. Google Maps showed me two street names in the US: Bornholm Place in Mt Carmel, just outside Cincinnati, Ohio, and Bornholm Street in Elk Horn, Iowa. Elk Horn is the largest rural Danish settlement in the US, and houses the Museum of Danish America, which also offers genealogy research.

Another Bornholm is located in south-western Australia, a five-hour drive from Perth. According to a 1914 newspaper article, it's unclear why the name Bornholm was chosen for a place that was first called "Cold and Wet" (then Martyup, and then Yonga), but apparently the inhabitants weren't pleased: "the name was changed, this time to Bornholm, much to the disgust of settlers, who think that if a new name had to be taken they might have been consulted, and one with more character than the present adopted." (*The West Australian, 29 December 1914*)

Postscript

Every family has a story, and Bornholm figures in ours. I grew up with an image of this tiny island in the Baltic Sea, in my mind a mystical place where the jagged rocks and icy wind require an extra dose of *hygge* on either side of its short summer. But stories get lost when there's no one left to tell them, and when my Bornholmer mother turned 80, I decided to find out more about this windswept Baltic island of several generations on my mother's side of the family. What is this place that has captured the hearts of so many, but is sometimes forgotten on maps of Denmark, and how have identities been formed here? I decided that the best way of finding out would be to let the experts speak. This book is the result of organizing, curating, and translating this content.

I should mention that when I started, I had only ever visited Bornholm once – in 1988 – just before the economic slump of the early 90s, and well before the creative boom of the new millennium. I was just about to turn 18, and had been growing up in the vibrant metropolis of Yokohama/Tokyo, Japan. I wasn't sure what to make of the quiet, rocky island whose water temperatures, even in June, weren't quite enough to tempt me. And another thing: I'm half German. I knew it had initially not been easy for my Danish mother in the early 1960s to introduce to Danish friends and family my father, Friedhelm Hirschbühl, with memories of the five-year German occupation during World War II still fresh in people's minds. Especially as my Bornholmer grandfather, Hans Kofod, a veterinarian in Hasle, had been active in the Danish Resistance movement during the War. Finally, growing up in neither Denmark nor Germany, but in Japan, set me up for a life of rootless globetrotting, although I settled for longer periods in the UK, Switzerland, and Thailand.

Many had a pandemic project – this was mine. In April 2021, my mum, who lives in London, sent me links to Danish news stories about the 75th anniversary of the Russian departure from Bornholm. Wait, what? The Russians had "occupied" Bornholm? I realized that my knowledge of the history of this island was sorely lacking. I also realized that apart from a few summaries and some tourist information, all the more detailed information and stories were only in Danish. And that's how the idea for this anthology was born.

I decided to create a book for non-Danish speakers visiting the island, either in person or as armchair travellers. A book that gives you an idea of the place, that makes you feel you've learnt a little something, that goes beyond mere descriptions to really capture the island's essence. I hope it delivers, in keeping you informed and engaged, while being a concise and enjoyable read, showcasing the work of Danish writers. The book's separate chapters allow readers to delve into specific areas of interest. Each chapter reflects the unique voice of the authors represented, each with their own relationship to the island. Ultimately, I hope this book helps to put Bornholm on the map. And if you're already on the island, I hope it is a suitable companion for your adventures there.

Acknowledgements

No project is a solo endeavour, and I am grateful to the following people for enabling me to create this book.

The Danish fund, Jorck's Fond (Konsul George Jorck og Hustru Emma Jorck's Fond), for providing financial support.

Jules Horne of texthouse.co.uk for invaluable advice, meticulous editing, and layout expertise.

Peter Reinhold Kyhl for sharing some of the in-depth genealogy research he has conducted into the Bornholm branch of our family.

The warm, friendly, and interested people I met on Bornholm who were always up for a chat. There are, of course, too many to mention, but special shout-outs go to the very first people I met when I visited the island with this project vaguely in mind, in November 2021, and whose kindness and helpfulness have stuck with me and set the tone: Christina Svensson, Jette Jensen, and Janni Grahn.

The owners of Restaurant Kokkenberg, who spontaneously lent me an old book listing the previous owners of houses in Sandvig, enabling me to trace the steps of my great-great-grandfather, August Wilhelmsson Lundgren (1864–1957), in the village. *Den gamle Lundgren* (old Lundgren), as he was affectionately known, had his *købmandsbutik,* or general store/corner shop, where Kokkenberg is now.

Reminiscent of a recurring theme in this book, Lundgren was born in Blekinge, Sweden, the son of a poor stonemason. The story goes that he wanted to emigrate to America, but his mother didn't want him travelling further than Bornholm. So, he went to Bornholm first, hoping he could earn a bit of money before making the long journey across the Atlantic at a later date. But as fate would have it, he fell in love with a local woman, Amalie Jensen, daughter of a fisherman. And Amalie, whose family had been on the island for generations, didn't want to leave Bornholm. So, they settled in Sandvig, where he ran a shop at Hammershusvej 2, and the rest is history. If he hadn't left Sweden for Bornholm, this book wouldn't exist.

For friendship and hospitality on the island: Anette and Peter Thunbo; Leah, Bent, and Lærke Lindahl; and Preben and Else Pedersen. The many people who took the time to answer my inquiries while I was still testing the waters, during the early stages of the project. Travis Lind Thornton, of Business Center Bornholm, for seeing the potential in the project, and encouraging me to stick at it.

All the contributing authors/interviewees – Jens Svane Boutrup, Niels Geckler, Rakel Haslund-Gjerrild, Bruno Kaufmann, Dennis Gade Kofod, Thomas Kofoed Poulsen, Lars Kofoed Rømer, and Henrik Yde – without whose original source material this book wouldn't exist. Thank you for agreeing to the translations and interviews, and for sharing your time and expertise. Thank you to Klavs Holm of Hakon Holm Publishing for permission to include Thomas's contribution, Chapter 3. Heartfelt thanks also go to Ane Ipsen and Malene Linell Ipsen, daughters of Henning Ipsen, for their encouragement and for allowing me to include Chapter 8, and to Ane for insightful feedback on the translation of Chapter 8, for help with her father's author bio, and for capturing so perfectly the themes of this book in her Foreword. I also extend my thanks to Ole Mahler for kindly granting permission to reprint the *Krølle-Bølle* images pictured in this book, and to Susanne Mahler, granddaughter of *Krølle-Bølle* author Ludvig Mahler, for valuable input.

Tiziana Dall'Antonia-Greger (cover design) and Anouk Hufschmid Hirschbuehl (illustrated map of Bornholm) for their eye-catching artistic contributions.

My mother, Susanne Hirschbühl (née Kofod), for introducing me to the island she so loves, for telling me stories that sparked the idea for this book, and for casting her eagle eye over my translations. It was my mother who sang me to sleep as a baby with a Bornholmsk lullaby, *Vizzeliroa*, perhaps planting the first subconscious seed of this project. As I was growing up, she introduced me to *Med Krølle-Bølle rundt på Bornholm (Exploring Bornholm with Krølle-Bølle)*, which her classmate and friend Jørn Leo Mahler's father had authored and illustrated, and which is now iconic to Bornholm. And when she learned of my deeper interest in the island, she dusted off and showed me the many Henning Ipsen paperbacks she keeps on her bookshelf in London, sixty years after purchasing them. As Ane Ipsen writes in the foreword to this book, her father's writing was driven by his longing for Bornholm. Similarly, my mother used to tell me and my brother Tom that, as a teenager, she wanted to break away from the smallness of the place in which she was growing up – yet as an adult, living in Germany, Japan, Malta, and now London, she yearned for the island of her childhood. This sentiment may feel familiar to many, whether it is a case of the importance of roots, or simply of absence making the heart grow fonder. Corresponding with Ane Ipsen, who lives in California, I learned that Henning Ipsen used to cycle to school from Hasle to Rønne in the 1940s, just like my mother did in the 1950s – and that they both wrote for the school paper. I am grateful for the opportunities for new connections and insights this project has given me, and hope that it can equally inspire others on their own journeys of discovery.

My daughters, Anouk and Manon Hufschmid Hirschbuehl, who were always interested in hearing how I was progressing, and for test-reading, despite facing their own challenges and being busy with their studies, projects, deadlines, and lives. My husband, Peter Hufschmid-Hirschbuehl, who gave me the space to unfold creatively, by taking over a large share of household chores, such as shopping and cooking, while leaving the fun tasks, such as feeding and cuddling the cats – there are always cats – to me.

The editor has made every effort to trace and contact all copyright holders before publication. If notified, the editor will be pleased to rectify any errors or omissions at the earliest opportunity.

Tina Hirschbuehl

27 Author photo by Manon Hufschmid Hirschbuehl.

Author biographies

Jens Svane Boutrup

Artistic director of Bornholms Teater since 2008, Jens Svane Boutrup (1973), writes, directs, and translates plays. He holds a BA in Theatre Studies from Copenhagen University (2001) and in Theatre Directing from Brooklyn College, City University of New York (2003).

Niels Geckler

Niels Geckler (1977), studied history and economics at the University of Copenhagen (2006). He has worked as a museum curator, a teacher, a historical writer, and a copywriter. He co-authored "Bornholm i krig og fred" (Bornholm in War and Peace) (2021) with journalist Morten Friis Jørgensen. Niels Geckler grew up in Odense on the Danish island of Funen, and lives on Bornholm with his family.

Rakel Haslund-Gjerrild

Rakel Haslund-Gjerrild (1988) burst onto the Danish literary scene in 2016, with her short story collection, "Øer" (Islands). She followed this up with "Alle himlens fugle" (All the Birds in the Sky) (2020), which was translated into French and Hungarian, and has consolidated her position with "Adam i Paradis" (Adam in Paradise) (2021), which has won a number of awards, including Weekendavisens Litteraturpris, and is available in several languages. Born in Roskilde, she grew up in Nexø, where her family have lived for seven generations. She holds a BA and MA in Chinese Studies and Literature from Copenhagen University.

Tina Hirschbuehl

Tina Hirschbuehl (1970) is a writer, editor, and translator based between Europe and Asia. She holds degrees from the University of Sussex, UK (1992) and Malmö University, Sweden (2014). She has worked as a radio and television journalist for the Swiss Broadcasting Corporation and is currently an editor for the Centre for Development and Environment (University of Bern, Switzerland) and the UN. Her mother is a Kofod from Bornholm, where the family goes back several generations.

Ane Ipsen

Ane Ipsen (1954) was born and raised in Denmark, and her last name is decidedly Bornholmsk. She has taught college English in California for many years and translated several books from English and Spanish for Danish publishers. She lives in Southern California with her American husband, who speaks Danish and occasionally Bornholmsk.

Henning Ipsen

Henning Ipsen (1930–1984), born and bred on Bornholm, worked as a teacher before launching his writing career with a book of short stories, "De tavse huse" (1956). He went on to write many novels, including "Ulla, min Ulla" (1961), "Midt i September" (1962), and "Orinoco" (1965), as well as another collection of short stories, "Kikkerne" (1963).

He also wrote what was considered to be the first Danish TV series: "Regnvejr og ingen penge" (Rainy and No Money) (1965), which depicts the life of a working-class family from Bornholm between 1945 and 1965. Later, he wrote countless book reviews and obituaries for the Jyllands-Posten newspaper, and he translated a great number of books and plays from English and Swedish into Danish. Among his close friends were the Bornholm painter, Oluf Høst, and the British playwright, Arnold Wesker.

Bruno Kaufmann

Political scientist and journalist Bruno Kaufmann (1965) has authored publications in more than 30 languages on modern direct and representative democracy. He is the Global Democracy Correspondent at SWI swissinfo.ch, the international service of the Swiss Broadcasting Corporation, and covers Northern European Affairs for the Swiss public service Radio and TV. Bruno lives with his family in Arboga, outside Stockholm, where the first Swedish Parliament was established in 1435. Bruno is co-founder and board member of democracy support organizations including the Swiss Democracy Foundation, Democracy International, and the Global Forum on Modern Direct Democracy.

Dennis Gade Kofod

Dennis Gade Kofod (1976) is a prolific author whose stories often combine realism with the supernatural and the spiritual; local legends with contemporary challenges. Born in Jutland, he moved to Bornholm as a small child, and grew up in the Balka beach area. He feels that he has deepened his senses on the island that also surrounded his father's childhood. His latest novel, "Power to X", was published in 2022. He now lives in Rønne with his family.

Thomas Kofoed Poulsen

Thomas Kofoed Poulsen (1976) is head of the newsroom at DR Danmarks Radio on Bornholm. He holds a BA in Political Science from Aarhus University (2000), and a Master's in International/Global Studies from Malmö University (2013). Born and bred on Bornholm, he grew up hearing his grandparents' stories of the Russian presence on the island, and decided to document eyewitness reports before it was too late. "Russertiden: De sidste vidner, Bornholm 1945/46" (Russian Days: The Last Witnesses, Bornholm 1945/46) (2021) is the result.

Lars Christian Kofoed Rømer

Lars Kofoed Rømer (1982) is an anthropologist who has made a name for himself as an expert on the "Underjordiske" (Subterraneans) on Bornholm. Having completed a PhD on the topic (2018), he is a sought-after interview partner and speaker and is active in a range of different projects on Bornholm's cultural heritage, including podcasts, audio tours, theatre, and books. He also works on the organizing committee of the political festival held annually on the island, Folkemødet.

Henrik Yde

Henrik Yde (1950), dr.phil., is Denmark's leading expert on Martin Andersen Nexø. He published a comprehensive biography of Nexø in 2019 – "NEXØ: Martin Andersen Nexøs liv og værk" (NEXØ: The Life and Letters of Martin

Andersen Nexø) – winning the prestigious Georg Brandes prize. The nationwide Jyllands-Posten newspaper described the tome as being a "thorough, generous, and beautiful" biography that should become a "standard work on one of the most significant authors in Danish literary history."

28 Danish resistance fighters during World War II. Hasle
Battalion, led by veterinarian Hans Kofod (far left). Only while
researching for this project did I learn how much Hans, my
grandfather, did for the community. Among other things, he
was instrumental in organizing a bust of King Christian X to be
created by sculptor Viktor Kvederis and erected in Hasle. Photo:
Family archive of Susanne Hirschbühl (née Kofod).

If you've enjoyed this book and would like to learn more about the production team's creative work, please visit:

www.bornholmreader.com
www.flamepointpress.com
www.tinahirschbuehl.com
www.juleshorne.com
www.texthouse.co.uk
www.anoukhh.art

If you're inspired to plan your next holiday, here are some helpful links as a starting-point:

To visit the island's tourism board website, Destination Bornholm, go to https://bornholm.info/en/.

To learn more about things to do and places to visit on the island, see the photography-based magazine and website, Visual Bornholm: https://visualbornholm.com/en/.

Happy travels!